NTO OUR HERITAGE OF TOMORROW

Banker Dahl

of South Dakota

An Autobiography

by A. E. DAHL

FENSKE BOOK COMPANY

Rapid City, South Dakota

Contents

To My Grandchildren

Richard

Dianne

James

Sandra

Foreword

In relating some of my experiences to my associates and friends over the past years, the suggestion was made that I write a book to preserve these experiences for the bank and for friends and other bankers who might find them interesting. I considered the idea for some time, and recently I decided to give writing a try. The result is the story of my life and my forty-eight years as a banker.

One of my associates suggested I set down some of my thoughts on various banking matters, my thinking and reasoning, for in his words: "I like to know what makes a man tick." This I have tried to do. Many bankers may not agree with me on some of the things I have said, and I respect their right to differ with me. I have also included some of the humorous incidents that have taken place around the bank. These, together with the tales of some mistakes we have made, would not have looked good as news items at the time they happened. But with the passage of time, they may now be told.

I refer to other people and other banks by name. I do so because they have contributed to my experience in the problems that have come up or because they contribute statistical data for comparison purposes. They are part of my story, and their inclusion is not intended as any reflection upon either persons or the banks named.

When I was born I was christened Arnt Dahl. Later in my school days it was decided Arnt was the wrong spelling. It should be Arndt, so I included the "d" in my name. As I grew older I wondered why I did not have a middle name. So at a family conference my father said if I wanted a middle name, I could take the maiden name of my mother, which was Elstad. So I added the middle initial E to my name.

While I was working in the bank in Toronto, Lyman A. Fries insisted I should always sign my name in full instead of using initials, and I did. When I came to Rapid City, I had to sign my name to so many papers in the liquidation of the Pennington County Bank that I decided to do it the easy way and sign my name with the initials, A. E. Dahl. Since the name Arndt was rather an unusual one, at least in Rapid City, some people started to call me Art, and I let it stand. People familiarly now call me Art Dahl, but my correct name is Arndt E. Dahl.

My thanks to those who have been helpful to me. To my wife Agnes and my daughter Verley and her family for their encouragement and suggestions. To my brother Victor for his frank criticism and advice, as well as for the time spent in helpful consultation. To my associates in the bank for assistance in gathering facts. To Robert and Barbara Gunderson for their suggestions and review of the manuscript. To Beverly Linderman and Doris Horton for their hours of work in editing and preparing the book for printing.

A. E. DAHL

Banker Dahl

OF SOUTH DAKOTA
An Autobiography
By A. E. DAHL

1

My Early Life

I have had a full, interesting, and rewarding life.
With no outstanding background, except good parentage, I have been fortunate. When I was thirty years old, I had a good wife, a lovely daughter, some good experience, some debts, but no money. I was somewhat discouraged as to providing for the future, and it seemed to me I would be fortunate to provide a living for my family, but no more. I had some hard decisions to make, but then things began to break for me. I was at the right place at the right time, and I have been successful in a way I never dreamed could come true. Perhaps I have been lucky, but I have worked hard. When opportunity came I was in my early thirties. We saved our money and built the nest egg that has grown handsomely in the following years.

I was born on the kitchen table on a small forty-acre farm near Taylor, Wisconsin, April 25, 1897, the eldest son in a family of six children. My father, Rev. Anton A. Dahl, was a Lutheran minister. He was born in Norway and came to this country at the age of thirty. He first worked as a carpenter and later decided to study for the ministry. His first pastorate was at Taylor. He met my mother, Lena Elstad, at Osseo, Wisconsin, where her brother was a pastor. They married in 1896. My mother was born at Franklin, Minnesota. Her parents had emigrated from Norway a short time before. There was no question about it—I am a full-blooded Norwegian.

The first language I knew was Norwegian and I spoke no English when I commenced school in a little country school house, a mile and half from our home. I recollect my mother telling me I could use the Norwegian language outside the school room, but inside I would have to speak English. The entire community was Norwegian, so the teacher must have had a big job to teach us how to speak English.

My father served three congregations, and his transportation was two horses and a buggy. We also had, as I remember, three cows and a few pigs. I learned how to harness the horses and milk the cows. It was a very simple life compared to the life of the youth today, but we had plenty of good, wholesome food to eat.

One night lightning struck the church which was near our home and burned it to the ground. It was the first big fire I had seen, and I still remember it vividly. There was a bitter fight among the members of the congregation about rebuilding the church at the same place or building it in Taylor. My father was in the middle, but he was a great diplomat, and the church was rebuilt on the same spot. A couple of years later the church was struck by lightning, and burned to the ground a second time. My father felt, however, that since he had served the congregation for thirteen years, he should move. I was now eleven years old and had three brothers and one sister.

So in 1908 my father sold the horses and cows and we moved to Cando, North Dakota, living in town. This was a mixed community, and the Norwegians were in

My Parents

Me

My Birthplace

Confirmation   *In My Teens*   Navy

Home, Cando, N. D.   *Home, Ada, Minn.*

the minority. My father preached in the Norwegian language, and never did learn to use English very well, but spoke with a heavy accent. Life certainly was different. We had to make new friends, and my brothers and I had to take taunts of "preacher's sons" and "Norwegians," until we licked a couple of boys and life became more tolerable. When I registered for school, I was set back a couple of grades because of my limited education at Taylor, so I was always the oldest in my class from then on.

We had a much more comfortable one-story home. The attic was one large area, and here my brother and I built wooden trains, engines, and cars which we ran on wooden rails all over the attic. My father was glad to provide us with the tools so we would be busy at home.

My father was not happy here, so three years later he moved the family to Ada, Minnesota, where he had accepted a pastorate. I particularly remember we boys insisted on taking along a mongrel dog we had adopted and become attached to. Our first night was spent at a parishioner's home, and the dog howled all night. I have never seen my father so disgusted as he was the next morning, but we kept the dog.

I was now in the eighth grade in school and went on to complete high school at Ada. The school years were more or less uneventful, and I did not make the most of my opportunity. I was not a particularly good student, and I disliked many of the subjects that could have been useful to me later in life. I was very much interested in manual training and mechanical drawing, and in these I received good grades. It never entered my mind that some day I would be a banker. I thought I would enter architecture or the building trades.

During the summer months I had various jobs. One summer I worked at a sawmill in Ada. My job was in the box factory. Another summer I had a job with a road crew. We graded roads with horses and scoop shovels. Later I worked on a farm. I cultivated corn with horse-drawn cultivator. I shocked grain when harvest came. I remember hauling in eleven loads of bundles to the threshing machine one day, and how exhausted I was in the evening. With the money earned I started my first bank account. One day my father found my bank statement and noticed several checks drawn for cash at a restaurant. He suggested that when I needed money, I should go to the bank and draw my money, since it might seem to the banker that I was spending all my time and money at the restaurant.

My younger sister was born at Ada, so now there were four boys and two girls in the family.

My father purchased a Paige Detroit automobile, which was a mistake. He should have bought a Model T Ford for less money and had a better car. The Paige Detroit brought one trouble after another, and my brother and I spent considerable time grinding valves and keeping it running. My father never did learn to drive, so we did the driving. Why he bought the car in the first place I will never know, except perhaps because he wanted to please us boys. Father was generous in that way.

The first part of December, 1915, my father returned home from a trip to Fergus Falls, Minnesota. His face was bruised, particularly in the forehead. He explained that he was riding with a friend in a horse-drawn buggy. As they approached the railroad crossing, the bell started to ring, the horses were frightened, and he was thrown from the buggy to the pavement. He did not appear to be hurt very much, but a few days before Christmas he lapsed into unconsciousness. We took him to a hospital at Warren, Minnesota, and on Christmas Day he died.

My father was a very religious man. Home life centered around the church. He was also a kind man. I am sure he had strong feelings of love for his family, but like many Norwegian emigrants in this country, he seldom if ever expressed his feelings in words. Instead, he showed them by his acts. If we wanted something, he would aim to please us. He bought a piano so we could take piano lessons. I did learn to play the piano, but not very well. I wanted a violin, and I got one. Then I wanted to play in the school band, and he purchased an alto horn. I guess it was wasted money since I did not do well on any instrument. He was a thrifty man and taught us the value of a dollar. He was stern with kindness, and we learned to obey our parents. He was opposed to movies and dancing. I am sure my early background, simple as it was, gave me a solid foundation for the years ahead. To my father I owe a debt of gratitude.

Mother had always been dependent on Father. Now she was a widow with six children. The parsonage would have to be vacated before long. I do not know how my father did it with the low income he had, but he had over the years saved more than ten thousand dollars. This was in time certificates in North Dakota banks, because they paid more interest. He also left 160 acres of unencumbered land near Fairdale, North Dakota. When wheat prices were good, Mother received a fair income which was helpful. We never sold this land, and when Mother passed away three years ago, we gave it to my brother Victor, who had been so helpful to Mother for so many years.

Mother decided to remain at Ada until the end of the school term and my graduation from high school. In June 1916 Mother decided to move to Toronto, South Dakota, where she had two sisters and many relatives. There was no rentable house, so Mother decided to build a modest home. My cousins dug the basement with horses, helped pour the foundation, and my brother Hjalmer and I built most of the house. Carpenters were hard to find, but finally we found one to do most of the

7

finishing work. I think the house cost about $2,500.00. It was a good house, but the plumbing was outside.

Toronto then had a population of about three hundred people. It is located near the Minnesota border between Watertown and Brookings. Most of the people were of Norwegian descent and Norwegian was the language commonly used. The town was surrounded by a farming community. The town had two banks, the First National Bank and the Farmers Exchange Bank. It had three grain elevators and a few business places along a short main street. It was a quiet, peaceful town and there was not much to do.

The first winter I worked in the postoffice, but the pay was low. In the spring I obtained a job as carpenter and worked on a couple of the large round roof barns common in the community. One of the last days of June, 1917, when I came home from work, my mother told me Lyman A. Fries, the banker, wanted to see me. I called at the bank and he offered me a position as bookkeeper. That sounded easier than pounding nails, so on July 1, I became a banker. That was far different than I had ever imagined, but it has now been my life work for forty-eight years.

I would have liked to go to college, but I did not know where the money would come from, and I did not ask Mother. Yet, all my five brothers and sisters have a college or university education. I think I will stop and tell you about them before I tell you more about my experience as a banker. My brother Hjalmer, who was about three years younger than I, talked Mother into lending him money to go to the University of Minnesota to study electrical engineering. He graduated and went to work for Westinghouse and paid my mother back all the money lent him. He died in his forties.

My sister Myrtle attended and graduated from St. Olaf College, at Northfield, Minnesota. She taught school for a few years and also paid my mother back the money lent her. She married Walter Aaberg, a lawyer and County Judge at Brookings until his recent death. My brother Victor was next, and he likewise attended and graduated from St. Olaf College, also on loans and his own earnings. He now lives in Minneapolis, and has been successful as a salesman of school books for the Webster Division of McGraw Hill Book Company. Next comes my brother Sophus, who graduated from the University of Minnesota as a civil engineer. He is now with the Milwaukee Railroad at the Union Station in Chicago where he has a responsible position. My youngest sister Esther also attended the University of Minnesota and graduated. She is now Mrs. Arnold Bonnicksen, and lives at Seattle, where her husband is Division Manager, Western Farmers Association, marketing seeds and beans.

By this time my mother's money was largely gone, but I cannot help feeling proud of her accomplishments and the great help she always was. She was an understanding mother and intensely interested in helping the success of her children. She passed away July 28, 1962, at the age of eighty-nine. We are forever indebted to our father and mother, and we all owe our success to their love and guidance in our formative years.

2

My First
Banking Experience

It was on July 1, 1917, that I first entered the doors of the First National Bank of Toronto to be a banker. I met Jerry Fries, president, and then retired from active work. He was waiting for me because he was going to get me started right. We found brooms and swept and cleaned the bank as it had never been cleaned before. He reminded me that anything worth doing should be done well. He had been a successful banker for many years, and his son Lyman was now cashier and managing officer. Gilbert Tuve was assistant cashier, and I was to be the bookkeeper. It was a very small bank. As I remember, the capital was $25,000.00 with $10,000.00 surplus and a small amount of undivided profits. The deposits were about a quarter of a million dollars.

My salary was $45.00 a month and out of this I paid my mother something for board and room. The checking accounts were kept on a big Boston ledger in pen and ink. Customers would bring in their pass books to be balanced each month. Shortly thereafter the bank purchased a Burroughs posting machine. It was hand-operated, but it was a big improvement over the pen and ink method. In between times, I would help at the tellers' windows.

Working in a bank proved to be very interesting. I now had a goal and I wanted to learn everything about a bank. In a small bank there is a greater opportunity to learn the over-all workings of a bank, and I never regretted having my basic training in a small bank.

Before the advent of the Federal Reserve System, every national bank had to have a small part of its reserve in gold. Although the First National Bank did not need to keep gold in their vault any more, they must have felt they did not want to part with it, and they still had a bag of gold coins totaling about five thousand dollars. Most of the coins were in $20 denominations. That was the most gold I had seen, and more gold than you will find in any bank today. Not long after that, the gold was shipped to the Federal Reserve Bank. I do not remember if they received full value of the coins, but I understand it was weighed and credit given on the weight rather than on the count of the coins.

At the end of the year they must have thought I was doing a good job and my salary was raised to $65.00 a month.

Since Toronto was a Norwegian community, it was necessary to be able to speak the language. At that time I could speak it well and much of the business at the bank was transacted in Norwegian. Since leaving Toronto thirty-eight years ago I have never had any occasion to use the language, so today I find it very difficult to speak it.

3

Navy Days

Came June 1918 and the draft of World War I was breathing down my neck. I was too young to register for the first draft, which included men 21 to 30 years of age, but now the draft was extended to include men 18 to 45 years. So in visiting with Gerhard Thompson, now in Minneapolis, who was one of my good friends, we decided to enlist in the Navy. We went to Watertown and enlisted and were sent to Omaha where we were formally inducted into the Navy. We had planned to be together, but we were separated, Gerhard going to Newport News and I to the Great Lakes Naval Station near Chicago. If there was a greener boy anywhere than I was, I would like to know who he was. I had never been away from home before and what I knew about the world was infinitesimal.

One day they split my company in half, and I was put in the awkward squad, which turned out to be a break for me. An officer came along and asked who could type and had some office experience. I raised my hand and I was transferred to the pay department. We computed the pay for each sailor and I was assigned one book of 500 names. The first few months I was on the night shift, working from seven in the evening to four o'clock in the morning. We were so tired towards morning that we did little work. Many of the boys did not care and the books were in a mess. Later I was assigned to the day shift. I had an inferiority complex, but having the opportunity to compare my work with that of others gave me more confidence in myself. I was also assigned to more responsible work. I must have done fairly well, because when I was ready to leave, D. A. McDougald, Ensign, Pay Corps, USNRF, gave me my first recommendation which said:

This is to certify that Arndt E. Dahl, for the past ten months, has been performing duties as payroll yeoman in the Disbursing Office of this station. During this time I have had occasion to observe very closely the conduct of this man in the performance of these duties. I am glad to recommend Dahl as a man who will perform any duties entrusted to him in a way which shows him to be honest, conscientious and an efficient young man. He is leaving this office for service at sea and it is with genuine feeling of regret that I see him go.

I enjoyed my stay at the Great Lakes Naval Station, and it was good for me to get away from home and mingle with other men. We usually had liberty each weekend and we would go to Chicago and see the sights. There were several service clubs in Chicago where we headquartered, and they provided entertainment, dances, and occasionally we were invited into homes for dinner. At night I slept on a cot at the YMCA for twenty-five cents a night.

There was a severe influenza epidemic in the fall of 1918 and many of the sailors died. I remember go-

ing to my quarters at night and seeing dead boys taken
from the hospital with a tag for identification tied to
their two large toes. Fortunately I was not sick, except
for some trouble with my eyes, which never have been
strong, resulting in a furlough home, when my eyes
were dilated.

The war was over, but instead of going home, in
March, 1918, I was sent to a Naval Station in Brooklyn,
and then to the U.S.S. Tiger. This was a Standard Oil
tanker that was converted to a troop ship. As we sailed
out of New York, I remember seeing the Statue of
Liberty fading in the distance, and naturally I had mixed
feelings.

The U.S.S. Tiger was a very slow ship, and two
weeks later we had crossed the Atlantic to land at St.
Nazaire, France. The crew numbered about two hundred. About a day out we were told the mail ship would
be coming along soon, and we should write our letters
home. Of course, there was no mail ship, but that was
the fun they had with us rookies. The crossing was uneventful but was rough at times. I was in the pay department and slept on bunks aft over the propellers. I
was seasick one day, but after that I was a pretty good
sailor.

We spent four days in St. Nazaire, but I did not go
any further. We loaded about two thousand troops for
the return trip of about two weeks. In mid-ocean we
lost one of the blades on the propeller, and there was
considerable vibration. The old hands spread the rumor
that water was seeping in and that we might not see New
York. They further reminded us of the Cyclops, a ship
lost in the Atlantic that was never heard from. Our ship
was very crowded and there was little room to move
about.

When we arrived in New York, we were put in dry
dock to repair the propeller. One day the officer in
charge of our department announced they could spare

one of us in the department, but we would have to decide among ourselves who could go home. My associate was Ralph Romer, who later became vice president of the Detroit Bank, and we both wanted to go home. So we decided to flip a coin to determine which one of us would be the lucky one. I lost and I made another trip to France.

The second trip was much like the first one, except that we went in with the tide in the afternoon, loaded, and went out with the tide in the morning. When I returned to New York, I was discharged and arrived home the ninth day of July, 1919. I enjoyed my thirteen months in the United States Navy. The experience was good for me, and I came home with a little more self-assurance than I had when I left.

4

Back to the Bank

I remember the morning I went to the bank to see if I had a job. Jerry Fries met me outside the front door. He did not welcome me back or ask how I had enjoyed the Navy, but got quickly to the point. He said they wanted me to go back to work. I would be an assistant cashier and also fill a vacancy on the Board of Directors. He said he would sell me ten shares of the bank stock for $1,700.00, which was about the book value of the stock. I did not have any money, so he took my note for the amount, and I would pay him out of money saved. I really felt important to be offered not only an officership, but also a directorship.

It was good to be back at the bank. They now had a girl to do the bookkeeping, and I found many interesting things to do. I was really interested in banking and took an extension course with the American Institute of Banking. I also read banking publications and tried to broaden my knowledge. I found things to do without being asked, and my associates were glad to have me help them.

Everyone was feeling good now that the war was over. Our bank building was adequate and good enough for the size of the community, but someone in the bank thought we should have a new building. Accordingly, an architect was employed to design a new modern building. Everything went wrong. Prices rose quickly and material was in short supply. The cost of the building was far above expectations. The tellers' cages were of imported Italian marble and everything else was the finest. It was a bad mistake. The new building cost about $25,000.00, which was equal to the paid-in capital of the bank. The new building tied up loanable funds and reduced our earnings. It was a lesson I have always remembered—that it is a mistake to invest too much money in a bank building.

The war had been over eight months and inflation had a good start. Farm lands were selling at inflated prices and there was much speculation. Lyman Fries, the cashier, also took the fever, and as I remember, he had purchased three farms. The price was about $200.00 an acre, and the down payment was small, with settlement the following March first. Many had bought and sold before this time taking out a profit, but by March first the boom had pretty well burst.

Lyman did not have money to make settlement, but his father, Jerry Fries, had considerable cash on deposit, and also with banks in Ivanhoe, Canby, and Hendricks, Minnesota. He also owned stocks in these banks. He must have felt that the name Fries could not default on their obligations, so he helped Lyman make good his contracts. It was a big mistake to speculate on land in the first place, but the second mistake was to pay for the land. As I will relate later, it broke both men and resulted in the eventual closing of the bank.

It was the spring of 1921 that I decided to get married. Lillie Quickstad, my bride, and I had been going together more or less steady since I returned from the

Wedding 1921

Our First Home

Hjalmer, Esther, Sophus,
Mother, Victor, Myrtle, Me

Mother's Home

war. So on April 27, 1921, we were married. I did not have any money, but we bought a small home for $1,300.00 with little or no down payment. It was four walls divided into a small living room, bedroom, and kitchen. The plumbing was all outside, including the pump. We had a hard-coal heater in the living room which took up most of the space. But it was home and we were proud of it.

Unfortunately, Lillie had back trouble. She took treatments at Toronto and Minneapolis, and finally had an operation, but it did not seem to do much good. It was a trying time, but we made it somehow, except that I was more in debt and had a hard time to make ends meet. At that time there was no restriction on borrowing money from the bank in which you were employed, so I borrowed perhaps much more than I was entitled to from the bank. Today no officer of a bank can borrow more than $2,500.00 from the bank that employs him, and the loan must first have the approval of the board of directors.

Three years later, our only child, Verley, was born on July 18, 1924. Lillie seemed to have improved in health. We had a common interest, and life became more enjoyable. Verley is now Mrs. Harris Torgerson, and lives in Los Angeles. She and her husband have two children, Richard and Dianne.

The economy was bad, prices were low, and many farmers were in trouble. Lyman was not the banker his father was, and I sometimes thought he was more interested in his farm adjoining Toronto than in the bank. Matters of importance at the bank were not attended to properly. His desk was one big mess. When I had spare time, I tried to clean up his desk, write letters for him, write past due loan letters, and present him with the letters to sign. If he agreed with what I had written, he would sign them, and those he did not agree with went into the wastebasket.

The cash reserves of the bank were running low and we had to borrow from the Federal Reserve Bank by rediscounting notes. I would usually handle this by finding good notes with ample security and send them to the Federal Reserve Bank for credit. Some were returned because of inadequate security or improper financial statements, and then I had to try to find others to replace the returned notes. It was very good experience for me.

Bankers in those days lent largely on the reputation of the borrower. Perhaps they would obtain a statement of the borrower, and most often not. They thought they knew all the farmers in the small community. So when we had to rediscount the notes, I often had to go out to the farmer and obtain a financial statement to make the paper acceptable. Men who had been reliable and had a good reputation were slipping financially. Many losses had developed, and the bank did not have the reserves and undivided profits to charge the bad notes out. The bank was in bad shape financially.

The bank examiners criticized the bank severely. I remember the directors would meet with the examiner in the directors' room in the evening. It was decided that the bank had to have a 100% assessment, which meant the stockholders had to raise $25,000.00 to remove the bad paper from the bank. This was possibly about the year 1924. By this time I had paid Jerry $600.00 on my note with a balance of $1,100.00. I did not have any money to pay an assessment, so I surrendered my stock to Jerry and he cancelled the note and paid the assessment on the stock. Well, I had lost the first $600.00 I had earned, but I never felt bad about it. I had valuable experience, probably better than I could have had if I had gone to college. Jerry and Lyman owned more than half of the stock and the assessment was paid.

The First National Bank was a good, conservative bank before the war, and usually had more cash than could be loaned at Toronto. So the bank bought about $20,000.00 in notes from a bank at Garretson, South Dakota, which was operated by a former employee. We trusted this man and bought the notes without proper investigation. When the Garretson bank closed, we had to take over the collection of the notes and found them worthless. There was one borrower in Nebraska, and I was sent to see if I could collect it. Another lived north of Fargo, and I drove there in my old Model T automobile. This loan was also bad. The bank lost most of the $20,000.00, which was one of the reasons for the assessments.

The bank had also purchased some notes from a bank in North Dakota. When the notes came due we would draw a draft on the North Dakota bank. The first drafts were paid, but finally they refused to pay any more, and as I remember, our bank lost another four or five thousand dollars.

We had several foreclosures. I remember one of about $2,000.00 secured by a mortgage on hogs. We discovered many of the hogs had been sold, the security was inadequate, and the borrower had filed bankruptcy. I was to handle the foreclosure, and the attorney for the bankrupt was present for the sale. He told me I could not foreclose, but I bluffed him, held the sale, and took possession of the remaining hogs, but we lost several hundred dollars.

When conditions were so bad that a farmer could not pay, we often took a second mortgage on his farm. Then we later foreclosed the mortgage, and in the meantime we would pay delinquent taxes and interest on the first mortgage. So we may have started with a couple of thousand dollars, but by the time we got title we had double this amount in the loan and eventually lost the entire amount by the foreclosure of the first mortgage. This taught me a good lesson. If you have a bad loan, take your loss and do not send good money after the bad.

21

I have followed this policy, and when we have a bad loan we collect what we can obtain quickly and take our loss. I want our officers to think constructively, make new loans, and not have to worry about a mistake of the past.

We paid six per cent interest on time certificates and this did not help our earnings. We raised the interest rates on the loans to ten per cent. Our earnings were meager and did not provide earnings to charge losses to. Another lesson was brought home and that is that a strong bank should have good earnings. If earnings are good, the losses are not so hard to handle. Another mistake banks made in the years prior to the First World War was that they did not build their reserves and capital funds. They paid out all their earnings in dividends. The First National Bank of Toronto used to pay out $5,000.00 in dividends every year and added little or nothing to their capital accounts. This was another good lesson for me, and in Rapid City we have never paid out more than one-fourth of our earnings in dividends, which has enabled us to build our capital accounts with the growth of the bank.

There were no installment loans in those days and no plan was set up to pay the loans. When the loan matured, the borrower usually received a renewal and the note would remain with the bank for years or until the farmer had a sale. The secret of loaning money today is that the borrower must have an income sufficient to pay the loan on an agreed plan. Property never paid a debt without a sale or forcing a man out of business-- it is income that pays the indebtedness. A man may have much property and equities, but I would rather loan money to a man with a good income and less property. I remember one day Lyman showed me a statement of a borrower who showed a worth of $135,000.00, and he remarked that this was the richest man in the

*First National Bank,
Toronto, S. D.*

I Am A Father

*Citizens State Bank,
Castlewood, S. D.*

Home, Castlewood, S. D.

community. The worth was largely in equities, and a few years later he was bankrupt.

Mortgages were then usually made for five-year periods and in those days a national bank could not make a loan for more than this time. When the loan came due and the borrower could not pay, the loan was renewed for another five years. Today how much more sensible it is to make a much longer loan, but with monthly installments coupled with monthly payment of taxes and insurance. In those days taxes were often unpaid and impaired the loan.

Another job I had was to go out and clerk farm sales. This was usually a big event in the community and all the neighbors came. On small items the auctioneer would sell so fast that I had a hard job to keep up with him. And then imagine a real cold day with below zero temperature. I had my work cut out for me. After the sales came the settlements. Some paid in cash, but I had to take notes and mortgages from others. The clerk was important and it was an interesting experience.

In a small community like Toronto, the banker was an important person, so I was clerk of the school board, and I have been commander, adjutant, and service officer for the American Legion.

In the early twenties the Non-Partisan League was strong and most of the farmers belonged to the league. We got into one big mess. The league had a meeting and the speaker used the village bandstand, which was directly across from the bank. We also had a ball club. We had a local light plant, and the owner was out of town. His son conspired with some of the ball players that they would climb on top of the bank, and when the lights were turned out, the ball players would throw eggs at the speaker. Things really began to happen. The farmers blamed the business people. My brother-in-

24

law, who was a farmer, would not speak to his brother who operated a grocery store in town. They retaliated by going to other towns to shop. They were planning to start a run on our bank, but I guess those that were the most angry did not have much money in the bank. We lost a few thousand dollars in deposits and it hurt when we already were in a tight position. I remember one man came in to draw his money in a belligerent mood, but I had to tell him his account was overdrawn. It was a long time before things became normal.

Then one day our competitor, the Farmers Exchange Bank, closed. A town as small as Toronto should never have had two banks in the first place. At that time South Dakota was overbanked with more than seven hundred banks. Today we have 247 banks and branches in South Dakota.

You would naturally think that when there was one bank where there had been two before, the remaining bank would gain, but that was not the case. Not only were thousands of dollars frozen and lost in the closed bank, but the community was shaken to a point where the people lost confidence in banks. That was the story in Toronto, and instead of gaining deposits we continued to lose deposits and our troubles multiplied. Although we continued to collect on loans, we could not keep up with the withdrawals.

By this time I began to regret the day I decided to become a banker. I could not sleep nights. It was not pleasant to go to the bank in the morning and take in deposits from your friends and customers, when you had lost confidence in the bank. I did not have any investment in the bank to lose, but the thought of being associated with a bank that would close was not a pleasant one. I made my own classification of the assets of the bank into good, doubtful, and loss, and there was no question in my mind that the bank could not make it.

One morning I told Jerry Fries that if the stockholders did not put more money into the bank in the form of an assessment, the bank would close. I knew that by this time both Lyman and Jerry were nearly broke and could not possibly raise any money to save the bank. Jerry replied: "You are just an old pessimist." Why should I tell a man many years my senior that his bank was going broke, when he would not listen to me?

I decided I had had enough and could not stand it any longer. I told Lyman and Jerry I was going to resign on December 31, 1926, which was then two months away. They told me I could not do that because people would talk. I explained that the volume of business had gone down so that they could get along without me, that the only possible salvation for the bank was to cut expenses, and that one way to do so was for me to leave and the bank could save my salary. They agreed and we parted as friends.

On December 31 I received my last pay check of $150.00 for the last month. That was the only thing between me and starvation. I was in debt to the bank about $900.00 with no security, so I was worse than broke. It took guts to quit, and it was a hard decision to make, but I felt it was the right one. Incidentally, the bank continued to run about fifteen months more, and then was closed and placed in receivership. At least I had severed my connection with the bank before it closed, and for that I have since been thankful.

I had spent nine and a half years with the bank, less my time in the Navy and I was twenty-nine years old. I do not regret this experience since I learned much, and discovered many of the pitfalls in banking. I know what hard times can be like and I never want to see those days again. I am sure this experience made me more conservative and a better banker. Most of the bankers today have not had this experience. Jerry and Lyman Fries were wonderful people, and honest. It is not all their fault since they had to contend with conditions that were extraordinary. They are both deceased now, but I will always remember them for the things they did for me and the opportunity they gave me to become a banker. I know I am richer in knowledge and experience that has proved valuable to me in later years.

5

I Become An Attorney

In a town as small as Toronto there is not much a person can do with his spare time. A young attorney, Walter M. Aaberg, a graduate of the University of South Dakota Law School and former catcher of the Toronto ball team, decided to come to Toronto and hang out his shingle. We became good friends. He had the legal knowledge, but my experience in the bank was a practical knowledge. We used to visit together in his office in the evenings, and I was helpful to him in some respects. One day he suggested I should study law. At that time it was possible to register with the Supreme Court that you were studying law in the office of an attorney. He offered me the use of his books, and I began the study of law in his office. This was in the year 1924. I was determined I was going to be a lawyer. I set up a rigid schedule of study, allotting so many weeks to each phase of the law. For five days a week I spent about an hour early in the morning before I went to the bank, when my mind was fresh to study. Then on Saturday and Sunday I would review my week's study, and often in the evening I would be at his office and he would help me. I did this studiously for three years.

So when I left the bank I spent my first month reviewing the South Dakota Code and cramming to be ready to take the bar examination in Pierre before the Supreme Court in February. Since my money was limited, I got a ride to Pierre and shared a room with Peter Sorensen, representative from our county. It was a three-day examination in six sessions. The first session was a group of hypothetical questions. They looked hard to me and I was beginning to wonder if I could answer them. I sat perhaps half an hour without answering a question and I almost felt like leaving, but I had spent my time coming to Pierre, so I began answering the questions. The following sessions seemed to be easier and I felt much better about it.

It was about a month before I heard that I had passed the Bar Examination. There were eleven candidates, and five passed. I was second high. My certificate of admission to the Bar of South Dakota hangs on the wall in my office. It is dated March 7, 1927, and incidentally, one of the oldest in Rapid City.

Walter Aaberg married my sister Myrtle and decided to move his law practice to Brookings. He offered to turn his practice over to me, so I thought I would practice law. I soon found that people in the community did not look upon me as a lawyer, but rather as the boy who had worked in the bank. I did not make enough to live, but luck was with me and better things were to come.

6

Again I Am A Banker

One Sunday in July, 1927, I attended church, as I usually did on Sunday. Most of the time after the service I would leave immediately for home. On this Sunday for some unknown reason I stopped outside the church to visit. Bert Tollefson, brother-in-law of Carl Halvorson, Castlewood, South Dakota, whom I had known, also attended our church, and we stopped to visit. He asked what I was doing, and I replied I was trying to make a living practicing law. He told me that the Citizens State Bank in Castlewood, thirty miles from Toronto, was looking for an assistant cashier.

The next morning I drove to Castlewood for an interview with Carl Halvorson, cashier, and Dr. Vaughn, local physician, inactive president of the bank. Finally, Dr. Vaughn said: "You may have the job and if we like you, you will stay, but if we don't, out you go." So I was back in the banking business. The pay was $125.00 a month. I explained I was a member of the Bar, and since there was no attorney in Castlewood, I would like to have the opportunity to practice some law on the side. This was agreed to.

Incidentally, Carl Halvorson is the father of Russell Halvorson, now vice president of this bank. Russell was then three years old, and it was at a subsequent meeting in Minneapolis after his college days that I invited him to join us.

Castlewood is a town of about 600 people and larger than Toronto, located sixteen miles south of Watertown. It was a nice town and we found we were going to enjoy living there, and we made many friends. The community was of mixed nationality. After spending the first month at the Halvorson home, we obtained a home to rent, and my wife and daughter came to Castlewood. After coming here, Lillie regained most of her health and felt much better. Perhaps leaving Toronto and all the troubles and worry there was a stimulus we both needed.

The Citizens State Bank of Castlewood had gone through a reorganization and reopened on March 9, 1927. Business was slow and Mr. Halvorson and a girl were the only employees. The girl resigned and I took her place, so Mr. Halvorson and I did everything around the bank. Again I had to post the books, and in between times I was teller, janitor, insurance agent, besides doing many other duties around the bank. Business commenced growing and for about two months I had to work most evenings, sometimes to near midnight. Then we employed Minnie Roberts, who took over the bookkeeping, so we did not have to work so hard. At the year end, December 31, 1927, we published the following statement:

31

RESOURCES

Cash and Due from Banks	$ 46,505.76
United States Bonds	56,720.98
State and Municipal Bonds	15,500.00
Loans and Discounts	81,936.54
Banking House and Fixtures	10,500.00
Interest Accrued Receivable	1,573,65
Total	$212,736.93

LIABILITIES AND CAPITAL

Deposits	$180,187.28
Capital Stock	25,000.00
Surplus Fund	3,000.00
Undivided Profits	2,460.78
Reserve for Interest, Taxes, etc.	2,088.87
Total	$212,736.93

Mr. Halvorson was most cooperative and I had an opportunity to put some of my ideas to work. Most small banks operate on a cash basis, but I set up the books on the accrual basis, which would give us a more accurate picture of our earnings. We purchased automobile contracts and made loans on the installment basis, which was largely unheard-of in those days. We also made monthly installment real estate mortgages which was new in small banks. At the year end I prepared a detailed report of the assets and earnings of the bank and I had much enjoyment doing it.

We nearly got into trouble investing in industrial bonds, and many other banks did. At that time many salesmen from Minneapolis banks and investment houses called on us to sell industrial and foreign bonds. I read the Wall Street Journal, the Financial Chronicle, and other financial papers and I thought I was an expert on investments. The salesmen sold bonds like Insull Utilities which were rated AAA, but in the stock market crash in 1929 they went into bankruptcy and the bonds became nearly worthless. The bank invested about twenty thousand dollars in industrial bonds. I became worried at about the time of the stock market crash, and I suggested to the board of directors to sell all the bonds and take our loss, which was then very small. We did, and a few months later the market collapsed and many of the bonds dropped to very low prices. Our loss was only a few hundred dollars. I concluded then and there that industrial and foreign bonds had no place in a small bank, and that we had better make our investments locally in loans to customers we knew. Since coming to Rapid City more than thirty-one years ago, this bank has never invested in industrial or foreign bonds. Many banks do, and I believe most of them are good today, but I concluded we are too far away from the market and at a disadvantage to know what is going on.

My law practice, which was a sideline, was good. People were pleased to have an attorney in town. They did not ask me where I received my law degree and cared less. I was appointed City Attorney for Castlewood. I probated several estates, guardianships and mortgage foreclosures. I avoided cases requiring my presence in court and away from the bank. I kept a scrapbook of all the legal notices I had published in the local paper, and I counted fifty-six legal notices in the three and a half years I was at Castlewood. This gave me additional income. My salary at the bank was increased to $150.00 a month and I averaged about $250.00 legal fees each month. I paid all the debts I left at Toronto and we saved our money. I was able to purchase a few shares of bank stock. We were doing very well and we were happy in Castlewood.

In Castlewood I became acquainted with John Hirning, who was Superintendent of Banks in South Dakota for many years. He was now handling several National Bank receiverships, including one in Castlewood, and also the First National Bank of Toronto. One day I was standing in front of the drug store in Brookings when John came up and greeted me. He told me he was investigating the directors' liability at Toronto, and since I had been a director at one time, I could have a directors' liability. Directors in many banks which had closed paid thousands of dollars in directors' liability for excess loans made. I knew there had been some excess loans in Toronto, and it was not a pleasant thought that I would be saddled with a judgment of many thousands of dollars, which could be possible. My mind was put at ease one day in Castlewood when John Hirning came to me and told me not to worry. He said he was going on a vacation and by the time he returned, the three-year statute of limitation would have run out, and any liability I had would be outlawed. I slept well that night, and I was grateful to John Hirning. He and I became good friends. Before he died a few years ago, he appointed me executor of his will. Since we had a trust department, I turned the probate over to them, and of course I did not receive the executor's fee I could have had.

During these years there were many bank holdups and sometimes they were as close as the next town. During the time I was in Toronto and Castlewood, fortunately these banks escaped. I have never had this experience, for which I am thankful. There also were bank closings, and this made the people nervous, for which I could not blame them. I remember one day an elderly gentleman came to the bank in Castlewood and wanted to draw out his money, about $4,000.00. I asked him to come to the back room, where we counted out his money for him in cash. Then I told him that I knew why he wanted his money, and I did not blame him for being nervous about the safety of the bank. I told him further I knew we had a good, strong bank and we would be in Castlewood for a long time to come. I suggested he take his money, think it over, and assured him that he would be welcome any time to come back and reopen his account. A few days later he did. We did not experience very much trouble because we could face our customers and tell them honestly the bank was strong and solid.

It has always been my thinking that when a customer wants his money he should have it promptly without any questions asked. If the customer has been good enough to come to the bank and deposit his money, it is none of our business why he wants to withdraw it. A banker should be just as cheerful in paying the customer as he was glad to receive the deposit. Many bankers unfortunately are too inquisitive and will drive customers away.

In the fall of 1929, Mr. Luebke, an inactive vice president, died. The board surprised me by electing me to the Board of Directors to take his place. They further surprised me by promoting me to be vice president of the bank. Apparently the board members were pleased with my services, and this was their way of showing their appreciation.

One day while I was visiting with one of the young men at the grocery store, he indicated a desire to sell me a course of study in Higher Accounting with the LaSalle Extension University. Since he had never sent in a lesson, this was possible. Having spent three years studying law, and being used to home study, I bought the course for half price. I completed the course and received a diploma in Higher Accountancy. I had plans to take the examination for Certified Public Accountant, but about this time I left Castlewood and became so busy with my new work that I never did take the examination. I learned much from the study and it has been helpful to me in later years.

Deposits grew slowly and on December 31, 1929, they were $212,156.08. After the stock market crash we felt the effects in South Dakota, and on December

31, 1930, the deposits had dropped to $188,294.60. The earnings of the bank were good, and at the end of 1930, my last year in Castlewood, we had increased the surplus fund to $10,000.00 and had undivided profits of $4,964.03. In addition, the bank had paid dividends totaling $6,750.00 in the four-year period.

I have never been very active in politics, but in a small community you are often given appointments and asked to serve in various capacities. In 1930 I was elected secretary of the Republican County organization for Hamlin County. I became acquainted with many people I had not met before. Included were Warren Green and E. A. Ruden, who lived in another part of the county. When the election was held, Warren Green, a dark horse, was elected Governor of South Dakota. He appointed E. A. Ruden Superintendent of Banks. Here is where my acquaintance with these men changed the course of my life.

I had always thought I would like to be a bank examiner. There was something interesting and appealing to me to be able to examine banks and learn about banks generally. So I wrote Mr. Ruden and asked if he had an opening in his department for an examiner. Immediately I received his reply—he would be glad to give me a position as bank examiner and the salary was $225.00 a month. Now this was quite a little less than I was earning from my bank salary and law practice. There is nothing permanent about a political appointment, and I realized that the position could be terminated. Nevertheless, I wanted to be a bank examiner and learn all I could, and I did not look upon it as a permanent job, but one that could lead to a better position in some other bank.

My wife did not receive the news with any enthusiasm. She felt that we were doing very well in Castlewood and preferred I retain my present position. She was a very considerate and understanding person, and said it was for me to decide, and she would be agreeable and happy with my decision. It was a hard decision to make, but I guess when you want to do something very much, the salary and possible tenure did not matter so much, so I accepted the position.

One morning I walked into the office of Mr. Halvorson and told him I was leaving. Tears came to his eyes, and he said he was very sorry to hear the news. He remarked it had been so nice to work with me, since I was willing to share some of the responsibilities and decisions, but now he would have to carry the full load again. Carl is now deceased. I remember him as a wonderful friend. He contributed to my education as a banker, and for this I will always be grateful.

7

I Am A Bank Examiner

On March 17, 1931, I received my appointment as a bank examiner for South Dakota. We decided to continue to live in Castlewood, since much of my work would be in the eastern part of the state. I left for Pierre to report for my new position. My first assignment was with Francis Barber, one of the veteran examiners on the force, who was going to train me for my new job. The first bank we examined was at Seneca, a crossroad town near Faulkton. It was so small a town that it should never have had a bank in the first place. The deposits were about $50,000.00 and it was impossible to make any money. Later it failed.

I kept a diary of the time spent with the banking department, listing the banks I examined, their size, and making comments on the condition of the bank. I still have this diary. The second bank we examined was the Faulk County State Bank in Faulkton. This was a good bank, and it is still in business serving the people of the community. We journeyed on to the

Black Hills and examined banks in Spearfish, Sturgis, and New Underwood. Later I was assigned to work with Steve Anderson. In two months we had examined twenty-six banks, mostly small ones.

On May 20 I commenced working alone, and the first bank I went to was the Farmers State Bank in Kranzburg, a sound bank still doing business. I successively examined banks in Elkton, Sinai, Hazel, Volga, DeSmet, Flandreau, Sioux Falls, Humbolt, Toronto, and Bruce. Then on July 20 I was called to go to Waverly to a bank which was in bad condition, with orders to close the bank unless corrections were made. It was a very small bank with $61,943.00 in deposits, over half of which was the deposit of the school district. After the examination and a conference with the attorneys for the bank, I ordered the bank closed. Not a very pleasant situation.

I enjoyed my work and found it very interesting. I found many banks in excellent condition with good management, and today they are among the many strong banks in the state. I made many friends and gained a large acquaintance with the bankers in South Dakota. My work as examiner gave me confidence in myself. I had always had an inferiority complex, but this experience increased my self-confidence. Before becoming an examiner, I used to go to bank conventions and group meetings. Prominent bankers were present and spoke about banking problems. I thought they were so much better than I. Later when I visited their banks I found that some whom I had admired did not measure up, and their banks were often run inefficiently and were in bad shape. I began to think perhaps I was not so dumb after all.

Many young men who have an inferiority complex need not have. It is when they test themselves with others that they will gain confidence. It took me many years to rid myself of feelings of inferiority. Perhaps the advice I gave to my grandson standing on the railroad platform in Denver, when he was taking his first train ride to the World's Fair at Seattle, may be of some value to a young man reading this story. I said:

"Dick, you have as many brain cells in your head as anyone else. You are just as intelligent as anybody. Now it is up to you to put your brain cells to work. Some may be smarter than you in some things, but in other things you may be smarter. The important thing is to have confidence in yourself. I had an inferiority complex in my younger days, and it took several years before I discovered I could compete with others on an equal basis."

He surprised me by saying: "That's interesting."

I continued: "Now when you speak to people, speak up with a firm, strong voice. I dislike mumblers. When you speak with confidence so you can be heard, you radiate confidence. We older people are always impressed by a young man who comes into the office and speaks clearly in a confident, well-modulated voice.

"Dick, you will soon go to college and you will have the opportunity of a lifetime. Take it seriously and learn all you can. The subjects you study may not seem important to you, but they will train your mind to understand and grasp situations. I would suggest you take public speaking. There are many brilliant men who never progress far because they cannot express themselves intelligently and sell themselves to others. When you go into the business world, you will find many opportunities, and if you are prepared, you will succeed. Opportunity comes to every man. Many fail because they cannot see opportunity, are unprepared, or lack confidence in themselves. I have often said if I have been successful, it is because I was at the right place at the right time, and took advantage of the opportunity and worked hard. I have been dealt some very good cards in my lifetime. and if I deserve any credit, it is because I played them well."

On September 21, 1931, I was assigned to examine a bank in the southeastern part of the state, in a town of about 500 population. I soon found the bank in very bad shape. The losses were big and the reserves of the bank were low. After spending the day classifying the loans and assets, I was convinced the bank would have to close. I told the cashier I thought the situation was hopeless. He seemed surprised that a young man like me should tell him so. He did not argue the point, but said they would not close the bank and that I would have to do it. I called the Superintendent of Banks about what I had found, and he told me to use my own judgment. In order to be fair and not act in haste, we agreed the bank would open the next morning, but I wanted a meeting of the board of directors to go over the classifications again. I suggested he take a pad of paper and list all the loans he could collect that fall, which he did, but pretty soon he stopped. I again suggested the situation was hopeless and asked the directors to pass a resolution closing the bank. They refused, so I informed them the bank could not open the next morning. The officers asked about drawing their salaries, since it was the last day of the month. I told them I was hungry and I was going to have something to eat, and I would not take charge of the bank until I returned. When I did, everyone had been paid. You may be tough as an examiner, but you like to be human.

Later I was sent to a bank in the northern part of the state. The president of this bank was a very prominent banker. I thought this would be a good bank, but I was surprised to find that the condition of the bank was bad and unsafe. The banker did not pay much attention to me as he thought I was young and inexperienced, and it would be a routine examination. I spent four days in the bank with an assistant. I gave

41

him the most thorough examination he had ever had, and my list of classified and doubtful loans was a long one. In this case the stockholders had outside means and could do something for the bank to eliminate the losses. Before I left I could see he did not like me, but I made up my report and sent it to the Superintendent of Banks.

The banker was politically powerful and complained to the Governor. He cited one loan, a small one, and on this loan it is possible I was wrong, but he did not mention the many large bad loans I had listed. This taught me a lesson. In examining a bank that is in trouble, never list or mention the small matters, but concentrate on the large things that really require attention. I was sent to make a second examination in March, 1932. I walked in and thought I was in for a hard time, but this time the president was most pleasant. He thought, perhaps, he could soften me with words and honey. The condition of the bank was worse, and deposits had dropped without any reduction in the loans. The bank had acquired a large amount of real estate on foreclosures, and this was at best a frozen asset of doubtful value. This time I concentrated on the big trouble spots and losses, and never mentioned the many small losses. The bank was closed a short time later.

General conditions in South Dakota were very bad at this time, and it was a difficult time for banks and bankers. Many bankers were doing an excellent job and they are still in the banking business. I feel that nearly 100% of the bankers were honest men, but if they had been too liberal in loaning money in the past, the depressed conditions in South Dakota were more than they could cope with. If conditions had been more normal, many of these banks would have survived. Many bankers lost all their personal assets in an attempt to save their banks.

I did not uncover any embezzlements or find any

dishonesty among bankers during the time I was an examiner. I had a strong suspicion there was something wrong in one bank. Later events proved I was right, but I left the examining force before I had a chance to go back to this bank. The bank was in excellent condition. Everything around the bank seemed to be perfect. Although there were either four or five employees, everything centered around the managing officer, and the staff did not know anything. There were some code numbers on the notes for which I could not get any explanation. The earnings did not measure up. I voiced my suspicion to one of the other examiners, but there was nothing we could put our finger on.

Later this man was arrested for embezzlement. Unlike most embezzlers, he did not need the money, but took the money to invest in the stock market. When he was caught he paid back every cent, but he served a term in the penitentiary. He had taken interest collected on notes which accounted for the low earnings. He had also taken money from some of the larger accounts. One of his directors was an old man who had a substantial deposit in his account. On one occasion, this director made a deposit of $1,500.00. The banker took $1,000.00 and credited the account with $500.00. After the books were balanced and the deposit posted, he took the customer's ledger sheet and statement, inserted the sheet in the posting machine, and printed in the correct amount. The statement looked right, but if the depositor had balanced his account, he would have found he was short one thousand dollars.

In South Dakota we have a banking commission consisting of three bankers appointed by the Governor. He chooses the names from a list of bankers nominated by the bankers. One day the examiners met with the commission. I was critical of the real estate carried on the books of many banks as a result of foreclosed mortgages. Many banks had claim certificates against closed

43

depository banks. It was my idea that some effort should be made to have banks eliminate the items from their assets. After the meeting, Mr. Steve Anderson, one of the examiners, asked me if I wanted to be fired. He said I was stepping on the toes of the members of the commission, since they had some of these assets. Nothing further was said.

I know I am out of step with the thinking of many bankers in South Dakota, but I never have been very enthusiastic about having a banking commission in South Dakota. All the members are bankers and the public has no representation on the commission. The members are human and too many times decisions are made to protect their own interests instead of the public interest. If there was a need for another bank in the community where one of the members had a bank, you can easily figure out the charter application would not be granted. If I were a state banker, I would resent having my competitor on the commission, for he would have access to the files of my bank. I appreciate many outstanding bankers have served on the commission and have served well, but now and then the commission is dominated by one banker on the commission who is looking out for his and his friends' interests. My experience with the commission has not been good, which I will relate later. If we need a commission, then it should be a commission of public officials like the insurance commission.

My experience as a bank examiner has been most valuable, and it was one of the highlights of my career, but it was coming to an end.

8

Bank Liquidation

I was in Rapid City in July, 1932, examining a building and loan association. This time my family was with me and we enjoyed touring the Black Hills in our spare time. On July 15 Mr. Ruden came to Rapid City and he asked me to visit him at his room at the Alex Johnson Hotel. He told me the Pennington County Bank would not open for business the next morning. He asked if I wanted the position of receiver and examiner in charge of the liquidation. This was something new and I asked him to give me a couple of hours to think it over.

I enjoyed my work as an examiner, but there is nothing glamorous about the disagreeable job of liquidating a closed bank. I had always lived in the eastern part of South Dakota, and coming so far west did not appeal to me. I did not know anything about this part of the state, and I heard about a banker at Sturgis who was shot and killed many years ago. This was the Wild West to me. So I told Mr. Ruden I would much prefer to remain as an examiner and turned the offer down. He said he would appoint Mr. Young from Huron, who was liquidating a bank there, to the position, but he asked me to go to the Pennington County Bank in the morning and take the inventory, which is one of the first things that is done after a bank is closed.

It is not pleasant to place a sign on the door informing the public the bank is closed. I did not know any of the people in Rapid City, nor did I know any of the personnel in the bank, since I had never examined this bank. For the first time I met W. E. Shoberg, teller, and Earl Keller, bookkeeper. They are now senior vice presidents in this bank.

The Pennington County Bank was one of the oldest banks in the state and the largest in the west river area. George F. Schneider was president and he had been the managing officer of the bank for about forty years. He was now an old man, highly respected in the community. His was a one-man bank, and Mr. Schneider had not planned for successor management and had failed to bring younger men into the institution to carry the responsibility. In his old age he had become a poor collector of his loans, and refused to face his losses realistically early when he could have saved thousands of dollars by a firmer collection policy. Instead he let the loans drift, ultimately ending up with larger losses. It is a good example of how important it is to build successor management and bring in younger men to carry the responsibility. Mr. Schneider was an honest man, and left his personal deposit of more than $7,000.00 in the bank when it closed.

A mass meeting of the depositors was called five days later and was held at the city auditorium. The meeting accomplished nothing. There was much talk about reorganization of the bank, but the meeting was premature as no facts were available on which to proceed. I am sure Mr. Ruden knew, and from what little

I knew about the bank I felt a reorganization was impossible, but we could not say so at that time. Speakers at the meeting included Mr. Ruden, who spoke briefly, Theo. B. Werner, Walter Travis, and T. B. Thorson, local attorney. Mr. Werner stated: "I was a friend of George Schneider yesterday and I am a friend of George Schneider today." The audience responded in applause, which showed the high esteem George Schneider held in the community.

After the meeting, Mr. Ruden and I, accompanied by a couple of other men, proceeded to the hotel for a visit. I was ready to go home, when Mr. Ruden called me aside. He asked if I would reconsider and take the position as examiner in charge. He felt it would be better public relations to appoint an open examiner to take charge to cooperate with a possible reorganization, than to appoint one of his other men in liquidation work. He further stated that if later I did not like the job, I could return to my old job as an examiner. Then, to make it more attractive, he offered me a $50.00 raise to $300.00 a month. So I accepted. This is how near I came to missing an opportunity to come to Rapid City, after having first turned it down. Luck was with me.

The last statement published by the Pennington County Bank was on June 30, 1932. Deposits were listed as $2,180,556.57, and loans were $1,907,867.18. Capital funds were $252,604.02. The bank owed the Reconstruction Finance Corporation $386,755.05. On the day the bank closed, two weeks later, the deposits had dropped to about two million dollars. On September 8, 1931, the deposits were $3,071,982.59. The bank had lost a million dollars in deposits in ten months' time, and the loans remained about the same.

This loss of confidence in the bank was manifold. In the first place, we were in the depth of a severe depression in South Dakota. The bank was principally a livestock bank, and the prices of cattle and sheep had

47

dropped to low levels. There was also a drought in the area, and the economic situation in Rapid City was at a low level.

Another blow that had much to do with the loss of confidence in the bank was Mr. Schneider's connection with the Bank of Wasta. I believe he was president of the bank and a large stockholder. Unfortunately, he employed a man to manage this bank who turned out to be a crook. As the deposits in this bank were dropping, the bank sent to the Pennington County Bank notes for credit to meet the withdrawals. About $150,-000.00 of these notes turned out to be forgeries and totally worthless, and the rest of the notes were nearly worthless.

I remember one note for which the chattel mortgage stated the borrower had 2,200 sheep as security for the loan. When I interviewed the borrower, I told him that with so many sheep as security he should have no problem. He informed me he did not have 2,200 sheep; all he had was 200 sheep. I showed him the mortgage he had signed listing 2,200 sheep. He was surprised and went home and brought in his copy of the mortgage which showed only 200 sheep. The Wasta banker had left space in typing the mortgage for an extra numeral, and after giving the borrower his copy, placed the original back into the typewriter and added another figure making it appear he had 2,200 sheep. This is just one example of the worthless loans. Things like this should not happen, but Mr. Schneider, an old man, was not capable of making the investigations he should have.

The Bank of Wasta closed a couple of months before the Pennington County Bank closed. It shook the confidence of the people in the community in Mr. Schneider. If one of Mr. Schneider's banks closed, naturally depositors would be afraid his Rapid City bank was also in trouble, and the withdrawals continued at an accelerated rate. With the large amount of slow and uncollectible paper, the bank could not stand the slow run.

Bank runs are almost unheard of today. The Federal Deposit Insurance Corporation insurance program had has a stabilizing influence. It is mostly small depositors who fill a bank lobby during a run and make the spectacular news. Today depositors are protected, and this accounts for the absence of runs. A run cannot break a strong bank. Many sound banks that in years gone by experienced runs, based mainly on rumor, survived and are still doing business. A bank with sound assets has nothing to fear. Such a bank usually has adequate reserves in cash and United States Bonds to meet withdrawals. When the assets are good, a bank can always obtain assistance by rediscounting loans and assets at the Federal Reserve Bank and correspondent banks.

Rapid City then had a population of about ten thousand people. We were delighted with Rapid City and rented an apartment in the Hunt Lee building downtown. We decided to leave our furniture at Castlewood, because I did not know how long the job would last and thought possibly I would sooner or later return to my work as bank examiner.

Mr. Ruden appointed a depositors' committee to advise and work with me as examiner in charge. To this committee he appointed Roy Dean, real estate dealer; Edward Swander, of the Swander Baking Company; E. A. Lusk, publisher of the Rapid City Journal; Arthur Bale, rancher; Paul Murphy, rancher; and Carl E. Behrens, undertaker. It was perhaps proper that we should have an undertaker on the board to bury the closed bank. Roy Dean and Arthur Bale were the largest depositors in the bank, each with about forty thousand dollars on deposit. The committee had no legal status of any kind in regard to the affairs of the bank but acted in an advisory capacity, assisting the examiner in the valuation of the assets of the bank and the liquidation.

I had my first meeting with the committee in the directors' room in the basement of the bank. They were all strangers to me, and I detected a little hostility. Since they did not know me—after all I was quite a young man at the time—they perhaps had their suspicions as to my intentions and my ability to do the job. Mr. Swander did much of the talking, injecting a few barbs against banks and bank examiners in general. I thought to myself, here is a man I am not going to like. I was wrong, for we became the best of friends. I respected him for his integrity and ability and willingness to be helpful, and I am also sure that as time went on he respected me likewise. There was not much we could do at this meeting, since neither they nor I knew much about the actual condition of the bank. Roy Dean was elected chairman of the depositors' committee. We decided to meet three evenings every week until we could complete an appraisal of the assets and consider a reorganization of the bank. I felt strongly that the situation was hopeless, but if I had said so to the committee, they would have thought I was hostile to reorganization. I never did have to tell them, but intelligent men that they were, they came to their own conclusion, after an appraisal of the assets, that reorganization was impossible.

I soon found that being an examiner of a closed bank meant work and lots of it, and was far different from being a bank examiner. The first week we kept the doors locked, and everyone was busy inventorying assets and liabilities. Every asset, loan, overdraft, bond and property owned by the bank had to be listed in detail. Likewise, every liability, including the name of every depositor and the amount on deposit, was listed. When this was finished, there was no need for so many employees, and I had the disagreeable duty of telling them their services were no longer needed. Among them was Earl Keller, now senior vice president. I did not know Earl then and he was dismissed with other employees. Another was Loren Myli, who later came back to work for this bank.

It was necessary to reduce the size of the staff. I decided to keep G. A. Bailey, former vice president. He had come to the bank about a year earlier at the insistence of the banking department that Mr. Schneider had to have help. Since he knew many of the borrowers and depositors, he could be very helpful to me. Then we needed someone to keep the books, and I decided to retain W. E. Shoberg, who is now senior vice president of this bank. This was a good choice, and I soon found he was a very capable man. Then I retained Meta Kroschell, stenographer, and Alma Sorben, bookkeeper.

I was instructed by the political powers at that time to employ E. V. Youngquist as field man collector. I found Mr. Youngquist a capable man, easy to work with and competent. Since the bank was heavily indebted to the Reconstruction Finance Corporation, and many of the loans were pledged to them as security, they sent Mr. Hood to Rapid City to look after their interests. The RFC also hired A. C. Froelich, a former banker at Camp Crook, to assist in the collection of their loans.

At the time the bank was closed it had about 5,000 depositors and 1,800 borrowers. Assisting the depositors filing their claims was no small task. Most of the people were reasonable, but occasionally we had some angry depositors, but I do not blame them for feeling as they did. Mr. Youngquist and Mr. Froelich spent most of their time in the country to count and evaluate our security. Loans that had been good when made were going sour because of the low cattle prices and additional cost due to the drought, and that is a combination hard to beat. Ranchers owing the bank came in to see me, and some thought they would have to liquidate immediately. We helped many to refinance their loans elsewhere, and where this was impossible, we gave them a chance to work out the loans. Typical was perhaps Leo Ashland, who is now parking attendant at this bank. He tells the story. He came in feeling very nervous and expecting I would demand that the entire loan be paid at once. He relates that I told him to go home and we would give him time to work the loan out, and he thought I was a pretty decent fellow. My faith in him was justified, and given time, he paid the bank in full and ranched successfully for many years before his retirement a few years ago.

The depositors' committee met regularly, working hard, frequently until late at night. One member got so tired he fell asleep, but he woke up with a start when his dentures spilled out on the table. All compromises had to be approved by the court on petition and order. I remember the first time I brought a compromise petition to Harold R. Hanley, who was circuit judge at that time. He examined it very carefully and asked many questions. I was a stranger to him, and naturally he was careful to decide whether I had a good petition in the interest of the depositors. As we became better acquainted and he felt my judgment was good, he approved compromises quickly with few questions. He was most cooperative and helpful and I always appreciate the assistance he gave me.

On December 28, 1932, the depositors' committee gave a statement to the press that reorganization of the bank would be impossible. I further gave the press a statement of the progress that had been made. Since most of the good loans were pledged to the RFC, a large amount of the collections were paid to them. From the unpledged loans collected and the good bonds, I stated there was sufficient cash, plus cash from the sale of the bonds, to pay a five per cent dividend soon. I also reported that I had collected $26,491.70 from the stockholders on their double liability on the stock. Today there is no double liability on bank stocks.

9

I Am Fired

The election of 1932 resulted in the Roosevelt landslide. In South Dakota, Governor Green was defeated by Tom Berry, and I knew then that I would be out come January. Governor Berry appointed D. A. McCullough, of Sioux Falls, as Superintendent of Banks. He took office on Friday, and on Monday morning I was fired. I knew I would be replaced, but I did not know it would come so soon. I was replaced by Joe Schmid of Rapid City. I had known Joe, and since he had experience as liquidator of banks in the Rosebud area, I felt he would do a good job.

Roy Dean and the depositors' committee did not like it, feeling a new man would have to learn many details unfamiliar to him and would delay liquidation. Roy visited with me one morning and said he was going to start a petition for local liquidation. This was possible in South Dakota at that time if two-thirds of the depositors petitioned for it. I advised him against it since I had seen the fight among depositors at Watertown. Roy, himself a Democrat, had $40,000.00 in the bank and was determined to do so.

The Rapid City Daily Journal and the Gate City Guide took opposite sides, the Journal favoring local liquidation and the Guide opposing it. Soon a notice appeared in the Guide signed by four depositors stating they would oppose local liquidation as proposed by the Dean, Dahl, et al. group. I told Roy he would never succeed if I remained in Rapid City, since people would think I was trying to get my position back, and I was leaving Rapid City to go back to Castlewood where we still had our home. I left. That was the last time my name was linked to the local liquidation fight.

About this time I received a letter from A. C. Froelich that made me feel good, particularly since I was out of work, and I did not know what I was going to do. We had become well acquainted during his stay in Rapid City working together in the liquidation of the bank. He was now in Bowdle, South Dakota, and he wrote as follows:

It was with regret I read in the Aberdeen paper about the change in receivership of the closed Pennington County Bank. I cannot help but think of the hard work and long hours you spent there since you went in, and the benefit the depositors could derive from it had you been allowed to remain. I can say this, Mr. Dahl, those few months you were there are not wasted; they will come back to you threefold some day in the near future. The old place will not be the same to me when I come back to visit and not to see you there.

This letter turned out to be prophetic. The hard work I performed gave me the acquaintance that enabled me to become the managing officer of this bank, and I must say the rewards have been manifold.

I had my doubts the local liquidation plan would

succeed and I wanted to go back to examing banks. I had become acquainted with two of the examiners for the Federal Reserve Bank, working with them examining banks that were members of the Federal Reserve System in South Dakota. I went to Minneapolis and applied for a position as examiner and was promised one, but it would be a month or so before I would go to work. In the meantime, John Peyton became president of the Federal Reserve Bank of Minneapolis. He had been State Superintendent of Banks for Minnesota. He did not know me then, but we later became acquainted and he has always been one of my best friends since. He brought with him examiners from the Minnesota State Department, and I did not receive the job. I then decided I would wait for the outcome in Rapid City, and in the meantime practiced law in Castlewood, which helped pay the grocery bills.

Back in Rapid City things happened just as I expected. Depositors were signing the petitions, and then the opposite side would contact them to withdraw their names. There was a long statement by the depositors' committee outlining the advantages of local liquidation. One of the signers on the first notice, mentioned above, placed an advertisement stating he had never signed the notice. Then came a notice from the banking department that the depositors' committee was fired and a new committee would be appointed. The Rapid City Daily Journal printed an editorial entitled "They Are Fired," about forty inches long, criticizing the banking department and favoring local liquidation. Roy Dean wrote a long letter "To the Editor." A new depositors' committee consisting of Richard Ottman, John W. Hall, and W. E. Tompkins was appointed.

About this time Judge Hanley had seen enough. Since the liquidation of the bank was under the supervision of the court, he felt the fight was detrimental to the interest of the depositors. He called both the old and new committees to his chambers, and read to them a long statement he had prepared which said in part: "The knowledge, experience and familiarity of the old committee with the affairs of this trust have been and are valuable. I do not propose that the knowledge, and the judgment, that may be based thereon shall be lost to the depositors of the bank. He then ordered the old committee restored, and retained the new members, to work together as a depositors' committee. He further ordered that "Henceforward and in connection with this trust it is requested that not only compromises and real estate sales, but also expense accounts be submitted to the depositors' committee for approval." That was a requirement I was never asked to fulfill.

The Rapid City Daily Journal editorially questioned what happened to the dividend I had said was available before I was fired. The banking department said I was in error since there was insufficient cash on hand. I knew that, but I had planned to sell the government bonds and other bonds to make up the difference, but I did not want to make the sales before the day to pay the dividend. Why the banking department delayed paying the dividend I do not know, but to me it did not make sense to refuse to sell the bonds to make the funds available for the dividend. I appreciated having the editor of the Rapid City Daily Journal state in the editorial: "The fact remains that in late December, Mr. Dahl, the examiner in charge, announced they were in a position to pay a five per cent dividend; so far as we can find nobody questions or challenges the integrity of Mr. Dahl, who made the statement, and while others might differ with him on details nobody questions his general sound judgment." The dividend was finally paid in April, three months after I said it would be paid.

On March 22 the petition for local liquidation was sent to the banking department at Pierre. No word came back, and on April 4 the Journal printed an editorial "The Depositors Suffer" asking the Governor to take some action. The next day another editorial was entitled "Up to the Governor Now." On April 6 the editorial was entitled "And Silence Was Over the Face of the Earth." This was followed on successive days with editorials entitled: "He Knows About It" and "Another Week." The last editorial questioned the delay on the petition for local liquidation, and also asked why the dividend was not paid. The heat was too much for the Governor, and he wrote a letter to the editor on April 8 justifying the delay in acting on the petition and the delay in paying the dividend, claiming in part that I had misrepresented the availability of funds to pay the dividend.

The next editorial was dated April 10 and entitled "He Knows About It." The Gate City Guide had an editorial on April 14 entitled "A Few Questions for the Journal to Answer" taking the oposite side. On April 13 there was a long letter from D. A. McCullough, Superintendent of Banks, justifying the delay in the dividend and criticizing the editor for his tactics. The next day the newspaper answered with an editorial "Mr. McCullough's Hands." Back in Castlewood I read the Rapid City papers with interest away from the fight.

On April 17 the petitions were returned from Pierre, and counsel for the banking department stated that although sixty-five per cent of the depositors had signed the petition, there had been some withdrawal of names, so the petition did not have sufficient signers. The petition was filed in court, and an Order to Show Cause was served on the Superintendent of Banks to show cause why the petitions should not be approved. The order was signed by the Honorable H. R. Hanley, Circuit Judge. An affidavit of prejudice was filed against Judge Hanley, and Judge James McNenny of Spearfish was named to replace him in this action. The banking de-

partment opposed the petition and filed an answer on
May 3. More signatures were added to the petition and
other names were reinstated and filed. The hearings
did not come before the court until July 7 and lasted
three days. On July 15 Judge McNenny signed an order
giving the liquidation of the Pennington County Bank
back to the depositors' committee. The banking department ceased to have anything further to say about the
liquidation, and on July 22 the Superintendent of Banks
stated they would not appeal the decision. It was a hot
potato and I believe they were glad to get rid of the
Rapid City liquidation.

10

I Come Back
To Rapid City

On July 26 the local newspaper headlined my return:

DAHL RETURNS TO PENNINGTON BANK
     A. E. Dahl, Castlewood, has been retained by
the liquidation committee to act as liquidation
agent for the closed Pennington County Bank.
     Mr. Dahl is familiar with conditions in the
bank and with the possibilities of reorganization, since he was examiner in charge until Jan. 1.
His employment as liquidation agent was announced this morning by Roy Dean, chairman of
the local committee. Judge James McNenny yesterday signed a court order turning the institution over to the local committee. The state banking department, which had been contesting local
liquidation, has announced that it will not oppose the move further.

Why the new administration in Pierre should have
opposed local liquidation in the first place is hard to

understand. At best, being undertaker of a closed bank is a headache and usually a messy job. They should have been glad to get rid of it, but it was a political job. There are many things in life that are much more pleasant than the liquidation of a closed bank. Local liquidation was discussed by the depositors' committee when I first came as examiner in charge, and I offered to help them. The committee apparently decided I was working hard, cooperating with them, and dropped the matter.

Roy Dean spearheaded the drive for local liquidation. Roy was a Democrat so you would naturally think he would go along with the new administration. Not Roy. He had more than forty thousand dollars in the closed bank, and he was more concerned about his money than politics. He did not like the way things were going, and he was at odds with many of his good Democratic friends.

Well, after a six months' absence, I was back in Rapid City at my old job. This time I was working for the Board of Trustees appointed by the Court. I was welcomed back and I really did go to work with the trustees to make good. We spent many evenings making plans to expedite the liquidation and plans for a new bank in Rapid City. Since I had been gone during the entire local liquidation fight and had no part of it, I am quite sure the depositors and the community were glad to see me back on the job.

The Board of Trustees consisted of Roy Dean, Chairman; Arthur Bale, Paul Murphy, Edward Swander, and Carl E. Behrens. G. A. Bailey, who had worked for me before, was still with the bank, and I retained him a short time. W. E. Shoberg continued on the staff. E. V. Youngquist, who was also fired, was rehired to do field work.

One matter pending was the suit against the directors of the closed bank on their directors' liability. I had originally started this suit, but the Republican attorneys also had been fired and replaced by Democratic attorneys. Since the liquidation of the bank was now non-political, I retained the last attorneys. The directors were most cooperative and wanted to settle without going to court. On October 23, 1933, the suit was settled for a total of $183,690.27. This was the largest directors' settlement made in South Dakota. Other directors may have had larger liability, but too often the directors went broke with the bank, and could not pay. Very little cash was paid, but the directors turned over real estate mortgages, stocks, bonds, real estate, and waived their deposits in the closed bank amounting to $48,145.43. The large amount of deposits left in the bank by the directors at the time of closing proves they did not take advantage of their inside knowledge, but left their money in the bank with that of other depositors. They were honest men, but they had to cope with conditions beyond their control. The Rapid City Daily Journal headlined the settlement in big letters on the front page.

Many men accept directorships of banks as an honor without realizing the great responsibility they have. Directors may be liable for many things. They are liable for excess loans. If a bank has a loan limit of $100,000.00 and the bank lends $110,000.00 to one borrower, they are liable in a national bank for the entire amount if the borrower fails to pay. They are liable for paying dividends when earnings are not there. They have a liability for negligence which can take many forms. A strong board of directors who take their responsibility seriously makes a successful, strong bank.

When the bank closed it owned $143,737.50 in foreign bonds, and $167,214.42 in industrial bonds. The bonds were selling at substantial discounts, and some as low as ten to twenty per cent on the dollar. There was nothing we could do about it and eventually they were sold at a big loss to the bank and the depositors.

Now why should a bank in South Dakota buy foreign bonds in the first place? In those days it was quite common for banks to buy such bonds. The large city banks at that time had authority to help float such bonds. They had bond salesmen on the road calling on country banks recommending their purchase. They recommended foreign and industrial bonds as secondary reserves. What would you do if your city correspondent came to you making such a recommendation? You would perhaps rely on his judgment and buy something you did not know anything about. Can you blame George Schneider for buying these bonds under these circumstances? I don't. I remember attending the South Dakota Bankers Convention in Brookings about the year 1936, when Robert H. Driscoll, then president of the First National Bank of Lead and president of the association, severely criticized correspondent banks and bond houses for the promotion of such bonds and selling them to the banks. How right he was. The law relating to national banks has been changed and now prohibits banks from underwriting and distributing such securities.

Now let us go back to the inauguration of Franklin D. Roosevelt on March 4, 1933. The country then was in the depth of the depression. Many banks all over the country had failed, and panic conditions prevailed. All banks were hard pressed, and even the strongest and best banks were having large withdrawals. The President declared the Bank Holiday. Most of the banks reopened within a week, and in South Dakota 170 banks reopened. Banks in weak condition remained closed. The largest bank which failed to reopen was a national bank in Detroit, Michigan, with about one-half billion in deposits. This was the end of major bank troubles and the end to bank failures. A few banks have closed since, but they have been few and far between. Confidence was restored and the reopened banks continued to gain in deposits.

New banking laws were enacted by Congress soon thereafter. The Federal Deposit Insurance Corporation was established insuring deposits up to $2,500.00. Later this was successively increased to $5,000.00 and $10,-000.00. The double liability on national bank stock was removed to make the sale of bank stock more attractive. Banks were permitted to issue preferred stock, which if not sold locally, would be purchased by the Reconstruction Finance Corporation, to enable the establishment of new banks, and also to strengthen operating banks. Another provision was that the FRC could make loans on the assets of closed banks. These new laws were of interest to the depositors of the Pennington County Bank. I went to Minneapolis for a conference with the RFC officials and asked if they would be interested in the establishment of a new bank in Rapid City and make a loan on the assets of the closed Pennington County Bank. I received a favorable reply and communicated the information I received to Roy Dean.

So, at one of our meetings of the Board of Trustees, we discussed the possibility of taking advantage of the new banking laws, and decided to apply for a new national bank charter, and also to apply to the RFC for a loan on the assets of the closed bank to make dividends to the depositors available. There was much to do. We made a reappraisal of the loans and assets of the bank. We had to have the paper in better shape by new mortgages and chattel abstracts. By about the first of September, we had decided on a plan substantially as follows:

1. An application would be filed with the Comptroller of the Currency for a charter for a new bank under the name Rapid City National Bank.

2. The capital of the bank would be $100,000.00, one half of which would be preferred stock to be pur-

chased by the Reconstruction Finance Corporation, and one half common stock subscribed by local stockholders.

3. The par value of the stock would be $25.00 to be sold at a price of $35.00 to provide a surplus fund of $20,000.00, the total to be sold amounting to 2,000 shares.

4. The depositors of the closed bank would be asked to subscribe for one share of stock at $35.00 for each $500.00 they had on deposit, and to assign a sufficient amount of dividend they would receive to pay for the stock.

5. An application would be made to the RFC for a loan of approximately $400,000 on the assets of the closed bank to make available a dividend of twenty--five per cent.

6. The new national bank would purchase the bank building for $25,000.00 and the furniture and equipment for $5,000.00. They would also purchase good and well-secured loans in the closed bank.

We decided the new bank should be a national bank. We felt a national bank in Rapid City would carry more prestige, particularly since every state bank in Rapid City had closed. I was personally in favor of a national charter, having worked in both national and state banks. I felt there was less politics in the national system, and their examiners were more capable and more experienced, possibly because the state department never did, nor do they now, pay the salary to attract and keep capable men.

Then it was a question of selecting a name. We decided on the name Rapid City National Bank, but I never thought we made a good choice. The name tells two things — that we are a national bank and we are located in Rapid City. The name is not distinctive and we are often confused with the First National Bank in Rapid City. We finally decided to take some action and in 1961 changed the name to the American National

Bank of Rapid City, and later to the American National Bank and Trust Company.

The Rapid City National Bank would be a brand new bank, and would have no connection with the closed bank. It was not a reorganization of the Pennington County Bank. The charter of the Pennington County Bank would die at the end of the liquidation.

Application was made to the Comptroller of the Currency and he sent H. L. Wray, national bank examiner, and John Sweeney, assistant national bank examiner, to Rapid City to make a survey for the need for the bank, and also to approve the loans and assets we would purchase from the closed bank. Prices were at an all-time low, so we were very conservative. We selected only loans we knew had very little risk. We approved about $150,000.00 in loans, but when the bank opened they had been paid down to $114,482.68. Our conservatism proved wise, for every loan selected was paid in full.

The next step was to file the application with the RFC for a loan on the assets of the closed bank. This was a big task, since we had to pledge every asset of the bank, and the list was long. About November first, Roy Dean and I were called to Minneapolis for consultation. Judge H. R. Hanley accompanied us. Mr. M. O. Grangaard, vice president of the First National Bank of Minneapolis, was on the RFC Advisory Board. He was more interested in being assured that our new bank would open an account with the First National Bank of Minneapolis than he was about anything else. He was rather rough on me and asked if I could assure him that the loan would be sound and that the plan proposed would work. I assured him it would provided the RFC would waive the requirement that all real estate taxes on the real estate pledged would be paid. I tried to explain to him we could not pay all the delinquent taxes, since much of the real estate was worthless and it would be sending good money after bad. The amount was rather substantial, totaling about $20,000.00. He answered he was not interested in that, but wanted a straight yes or no from me. He stated further that as a member of the RFC Advisory Board, he had his own prestige to think of, and he did not want to hear any "ifs." What could a country boy do? We had come this far with our plan and I did not want it spoiled now, so I firmly answered "Yes." Later we received a waiver from the RFC on the tax requirement, and I was happy again. The Minneapolis office approved the loan and it was forwarded to Washington.

The next business was to sell the depositors the stock in the new bank. We had wonderful cooperation and most of the depositors having more than $500.00 deposit signed. I guess by this time they were willing to sign almost anything to receive another dividend. The unsold stock was purchased by the new directors. Since the stockholders did not pay cash, but only an assignment of their dividend when the bank opened, and the cash for the stock had to be paid in before the new bank building could open, I personally signed a note at the First National Bank of Minneapolis for more than sixty thousand dollars with the assignments as security. This was a big note to sign for me, having a worth of about five thousand dollars, but the note was paid the day after the bank opened.

The approval of the charter for the Rapid City National Bank came quite quickly. The approval of the preferred stock and the approval of the loan to the closed bank did not come before January, 1934.

Another detail to be handled was a petition to the local Circuit Court to borrow money from the RFC and pledge the collateral. My law training and experience, although perhaps somewhat limited, were very helpful to me. I decided I would draw the legal papers myself. It was a lengthy instrument and, after completion of the papers, I took them to Judge Hanley for his opinion and examination. He approved, but I could not file them until they were also approved by the RFC. I took the papers personally to the Minneapolis office, and after giving their approval, they sent the documents to a prominent law firm in Minneapolis, counsel for the RFC. The petition and order was returned without change, with the remark it was the finest petition and order of its kind they had seen, and I was told to go home and file it with the Court. Naturally I was quite proud.

Come February 1934, we had not received the approval of the collateral from the Minneapolis office of the RFC. I told Roy Dean I was going to Minneapolis and sit there until I could get the approval. Roy said it was a waste of money and would do no good. I told him I was not accomplishing much in Rapid City, and if I did go I could perhaps speed up the approval. I found an old gentleman whom I had never met before handling the collateral and he was just taking his time. I was at the RFC office every day and did everything I could to expedite the matter, but I remained in Minneapolis for about a month. One day he looked at a mortgage listing twenty steers. He asked about the increase, and although I felt like laughing, I explained to him that steers did not have calves. We finally received the approval.

On Saturday, April 1, I returned to Rapid City. I was interviewed by the press and made the statement the Rapid City National Bank would open in ten days. It was big news headlined in the local papers. We made it on the eleventh day.

There was much preparatory work to open a new bank. We had to have a board of directors, and of those on the board of trustees, only Roy Dean and I were willing to be directors. There was little faith in banks and the possibility of making this one a success. Mr. Swander finally accepted the directorship and said he would serve for one year. Carl Behrens agreed to be a director. Roy Dean induced Harley Johnson, local weatherman, to serve on the board, but just before the bank was ready to open, he decided not to serve. Harry Devereaux was suggested and agreed to serve, so we had the required five-man board of directors.

Roy Dean, who had worked so hard and taken the beatings in the local liquidation fight, was elected president, a position he justly deserved. Carl Behrens was elected inactive vice president. I was elected cashier and the managing officer of the bank. W. E. Shoberg was elected assistant cashier; Earl Keller, teller; Loren Myli, bookkeeper; and Frances Vincent, stenographer and secretary. We did not know how soon the bank would make any money, so our payroll was low. Roy Dean did not draw any salary. The directors suggested I should take a cut from the $300.00 a month salary I had been receiving from the banking department and under the board of trustees, and I readily agreed to work for $250.00 a month. W. E. Shoberg received $125 a month, Earl Keller $100.00 a month, Loren Mylie $85.00 a month, and Frances Vincent $70.00 a month.

Before the bank opened the supervisory authorities in Minneapolis questioned whether I was old enough and capable of managing the new bank. I have always looked younger than I am, so perhaps I looked too young to manage a bank in a city the size of Rapid City. They thought we should have an older man. I will always be indebted to A. C. Froelich. I mentioned previously he was field man for the RFC, so he and I became very well acquainted. He was a grand old man about sixty-five years old. He went to bat for me and told the powers in Minneapolis how hard I had worked to organize the bank, and they had no choice but to approve me as the managing officer of the new bank. They listened and gave their approval.

Mr. Shoberg had done a good job working for me in the liquidation job and I appreciated his ability, so there was no question about his employment as assistant cash-

69

ier. It may be of interest how I became acquainted with Earl Keller. Shortly after the bank closed and I had discharged him as an employee of the Pennington County Bank, he decided to go back to his home in Iowa. Short of money, he was going to hitchhike, and since I was going to drive to Pierre, I invited him to ride with me. We became acquainted and I was impressed with Earl. So when we opened the bank, he was invited to join the new bank. In the meantime he had returned to Rapid City and worked at the First National Bank in Rapid City before joining us.

Loren Myli had also worked in the Pennington County Bank, and was let out with the rest of the employees. Shoberg and Keller knew him well as a very competent man, and we offered him the position as bookkeeper. Roy Dean recommended Frances Vincent, which was also a very good choice. The remarkable thing is that Shoberg, Keller, Frances and I have worked together continuously since the bank opened. Loren Myli resigned within a few years to go into the retail hardware business at Wells, Minnesota. If he had remained, he would now be one of our top officers.

We were ready to open for business, but first we had to have a Certificate of Authority from Washington. We had planned to open Monday, April 9. About Thursday , I called Washington about the delay, and I was told rather sharply that the Rapid City National Bank was not the only bank ready to open, and we would have to wait. The certificate came and we opened for business April 11, 1934.

11

Rapid City National Bank

It was a great day for me. My lifelong ambition to manage a bank and put my own ideas to work was being realized. I had every confidence I could do the job, and I was optimistic we would have a sound, profitable bank. Yet, there was a tinge of nervousness.

The Rapid City Daily Journal on Monday headlined the opening of the bank in big black letters across the top of the front page:

RAPID CITY NATIONAL BANK TO OPEN FOR BUSINESS HERE ON WEDNESDAY MORNING

It was announced that the new Rapid City National Bank will open for business onWednesday morning, April 11, at nine o'clock in the quarters formerly occupied by the old Pennington County Bank.

The new bank will be a national bank under the supervision of the comptroller of the currency. As a national bank, it automatically becomes a member of the Federal Deposit Insurance Cor-

71

portation, insuring deposits up to $2,500 in accordance with the banking act of 1933. It will also be a member of the Federal Reserve System. Directors of the new Rapid City National Bank will consist of Carl E. Behrens, H. J. Devereaux, Edward H. Swander, Roy Dean, and A. E. Dahl. The active personnel of the bank will consist of Mr. Dahl, cashier, who will be managing officer. Mr. Dahl has been in the banking business for the past 16 years and before going with the banking department was vice president of the Citizens State Bank, Castlewood. At the time of the closing of the Pennington County Bank, Mr. Dahl was appointed examiner in charge, and when the bank was taken over by local liquidation, was appointed liquidating agent for the board of trustees.

Mr. Shoberg, assistant cashier, has been a resident of Rapid City for the last eight years. Earl Keller, who will be teller in the new bank, has been a resident for the past five years. Loren O. Myli, lately of Bismarck, N. D., but formerly of Rapid City, will be bookkeeper. Miss Frances Vincent, Rapid City, will be stenographer.

The new bank will have capitalization of $100,-000. Half of that sum was subscribed by the Reconstruction Finance Corporation as preferred stock and the other half was subscribed by the people of Rapid City and surrounding community as common stock. A surplus of $20,000 has been paid in, making a total capitalization of $120,000.

An advertisement of the Rapid City National Bank the same day stated in part:

The Board of Directors believe the new bank is commencing business under favorable conditions. Rapid City, a growing city with its large trade territory, has a sufficient volume of trade to support two good banks. The release of deposits from the Pennington County Bank will start the new bank with a fair volume of deposits that would ordinarily take considerable time to build. Likewise, the new bank will have some loans and earnings from the start. It is starting business when prices and values are on the lowest levels, which will assure loans made on this basis as sound loans. With improving conditions, the new bank will be ready to enjoy the benefits therefrom.

The directors and officers do not expect any phenomenal growth of deposits and business of the bank, but it is their aim to build the bank on a sound foundation, progressing slowly, carefully, on good business principles. It is their desire to build a bank that can be of the best possible service to Rapid City and surrounding community, enjoy the confidence of the community, safeguard their deposits at all times, and assist in every legitimate way to give the community and our customers every advantage that any bank can give with safety.

That was written over thirty-one years ago. Little did we dream that thirty-one years later we would have deposits of more than fifty million dollars.

The opening statement of condition was as follows:

RESOURCES

Loans and Discounts	$113,557.09
United States Bonds	5,000.00
Municipal Bonds and Warrants	11,102.96
Federal Reserve Bank Stock	3,600.00
Banking House and Fixtures	30,000.00
Cash in Banks and on Hand	295,817.98
Total	$459,078.03

73

LIABILITIES AND CAPITAL

Deposits	$339,078.03
Capital Stock	100,000.00
Surplus Fund	20,000.00
Total	$459,078.03

The deposits were all in one account and represented a dividend from the Pennington County Bank, less the amount of dividends assigned for stock subscriptions. We had 302 stockholders. The largest stockholder was Roy Dean with 100 shares. I purchased 50 shares at a cost of $1,750.00.

We opened for business in the building formerly occupied by the closed bank on the corner of Main and Sixth Street, a half block north of the Sheraton-Johnson Hotel. It was a small building, only sixty by twenty-five feet. When built it was a beautiful building with much marble. The tellers' cages had the old style grill work in front of the tellers. We had a small vault for safe deposit boxes and also for the bank's use. The book-keepers were behind the tellers. I had a small office just inside the door. It was so small that my friend Clarence Jacobson described it at our recent annual meeting, "So small that Art had to step outside the door to change his mind." The directors' room was in the basement. The building was adequate then, but not for long.

At nine o'clock in the morning I turned the key and opened the doors of the Rapid City National Bank for the first time. There were a few people waiting and I remember one man saying: "The bank is open." We were not particularly busy, but we had a number of new customers. Many opened accounts from the dividend they received. We opened several new accounts. The total deposits received the first day was $88,471.10. From that day on we started our growth and the deposits never were below the deposits on the opening day. Although there were no restrictions on the dividend available, those that were withdrawn in cash were more than offset by new deposits. We started to make loans, but the demand was slow.

Rapid City then had a population of about eleven thousand people. Little did we know then that Rapid City was to become the fastest growing city in South Dakota. Today greater Rapid City has a population of more than fifty thousand people. If we add the population of the Ellsworth Air Force Base, located a few miles east of Rapid City, we have a population of about sixty-five thousand people.

Rapid City is a beautiful city with wide streets and lovely trees. It is located on the east edge of the Black Hills, and is in the western part of the state. The Black Hills really should be called Black Mountains. It is an area about one hundred miles long and about sixty miles wide. It has several mountains, including Harney Peak, with an elevation of 7,242 feet, the highest mountain between the Atlantic Ocean and the Rocky Mountains. The mountains are a distinct group and the oldest elevations on the continent. The Black Hills National Forest covers nearly the entire Black Hills area.

The Park is a preserve for large game animals native to this area. About 100 buffaloes, 300 elk and 400 deer graze in the park under natural conditions. There are also rare Rocky Mountain goats, Big Horn sheep, and a variety of other wild animals and birds.

The lakes of the Black Hills are largely man--made. The largest and newest is Pactola Lake about twenty miles west of Rapid City. Most famous is Sylvan Lake, man-made and bordered on three sides by high granite cliffs. The clear, spring-fed lake produces reflections which suggested the name "Mirror of the Skies." There are many smaller lakes, all fed by streams and lakes, which are popular for fishing.

The scenic beauty of the Black Hills is of endless variety. Outstanding is the Needles Highway, bordered by granite monoliths. The route is noted for skilled highway construction as well as for scenic panoramas. The Mount Rushmore National Memorial is located about twenty-five miles from Rapid City. Sculptured by Gutzon Borglum, it is known as the "Shrine of Democracy." The Memorial is noted for the faithfulness with which the sculptor transmitted to this 6,000-foot granite mountain the facial features of Washington, Jefferson, Theodore Roosevelt and Lincoln. It is visited by a million people each year.

Also located in the Black Hills is the State Game Lodge, which became famous as the summer residence of President Coolidge, and more recently as a stopping place for President Eisenhower.

In the northern hills is Deadwood, early frontier town noted for the gold rush of the Seventies. Nearby is the city of Lead, the home of the Homestake Gold Mine, the largest gold mine on the continent. Nearby is Terry Peak with an elevation of 7,000 feet, used by skiers in the winter. The chair lift to the peak is a summer attraction.

In the southern hills is Hot Springs with its natural warm springs. Custer, with an elevation of 5,000 feet, is a favorite spot with tourists.

Rapid City, the gateway to the hills, has an elevation of 3,200 feet. The climate is dry and is neither as hot nor as cold as many surrounding areas. For a northern climate, it is a delightful place to live. It serves a large trading area extending into surrounding states. It has a diversified income from ranching, tourists, mining, lumbering, military installations, and is a wholesale distribution center. It has some manufacturing, with a large flour mill and a packing plant.

Although the other bank in Rapid City had been in business for about fifty years and was the only bank in Rapid City for twenty-one months, it did nothing in public relations to hold the deposits it received from the depositors of the closed bank or attract the many people who did not have bank accounts. When we opened for business, the community was ready for a second bank in Rapid City. Many former depositors transferred their business to our bank, and we received many new accounts from people who did not have bank accounts. The people soon found we were sound, careful bankers, doing our best to be friendly in all our transactions, and the trend started to our bank — a trend that has not stopped to this day.

We were very careful the first year and did not take any chances on loans and investments, because we did not have any reserves and undivided profit account to charge a loss to. This conservatism paid, the community approved, and deposits grew.

Other bankers were skeptical about our future. One day a banker from out of the city, associated with one of the group banks, made the remark to a local doctor that the new bank would have a hard time competing with the other bank in town, since it had been established in Rapid City for such a long time. Such remarks did not bother me because we were going to be successful. There were perhaps many other bankers that felt likewise. The man who made the above remark became one of my best friends, but I never told him what I had heard.

We opened a Personal Loan Department and, as far as we know, it was the first one in South Dakota. We made loans for personal needs and on automobiles on a sensible plan whereby the man on monthly income could pay by making monthly installments. Making personal loans in a bank was something new in Rapid City, and some unkind persons said we were a "Hock Shop" and a "Three Ball Outfit." The department was a success, enabling us to serve more people, and for many years we were the only bank in Rapid City making personal loans. This department brought us many friends and has through the years been an important part in our growth.

We started a planned advertising program, inviting business, and in those days it was somewhat of a rarity for a bank to advertise for business, and again we were alone in this field for many years. We invited the accounts of the small depositor, as well as the big accounts. We knew that there were so many more of the "'little fellows" and we had to have their business and friendship to grow. Advertising has always had a part in the growth of the bank.

One thing that irritated me was that many people in town called our new bank the Pennington County Bank. It was probably natural they should do so since we occupied the same building as the old bank, and people were not fully aware we had a new charter and were a new bank. So the first thing I did was to resign as liquidating agent for the board of trustees. E. V. Youngquist succeeded me and handled the liquidation from then on. I also asked them to move out of the building, and they moved to an office in the Elks Building. The bank was finally liquidated a couple of years later and returned to the depositors about 54% of their deposits.

So that the people would know we were a new bank, we adopted the slogan "Rapid City's New Bank" and used it for the first few years. Later we adopted the slogan "The Bank Customers Built," which we have continued to use up to the present time. We directors and officers may have had something to do with building the bank, but without customers we would not have gone far. We feel our customers, who have come to us in such large numbers, are deserving of this recognition.

The first examination of the bank was in November 1934 by Walter W. Olson, national bank examiner. He complimented us upon the progress made and said this was the first time he had examined a new bank and

78

found we were operating in the black. We had a clean bank and he offered no criticism. We had met our first test and it was a good feeling. New banks and branches started today usually run at a loss from one to three years. We operated at a loss for only seven months.

We ended the year with a profit of $701.42. The deposits totaled $741,173.31, more than double our opening deposits. Our loans grew slowly and at the year's end they were $166,456.33.

12

Nineteen Thirty Five

In the early part of our second year business had grown to where we needed more help. We wrote the Walters Company of Omaha, asking if they had some promising young man looking for work in a b a n k. Among the several recommendations was the name of Walter W. Pailing, and we offered him the position as bookkeeper. He had graduated from the University of Nebraska, and had had a little experience in his brother's bank. When Walt walked in I think he was so nervous that he did not make a strong impression, but we soon found he was a very capable man and were pleased with our choice. He continued to work in the various departments of the bank, and in 1955 he was elected president of the American National Bank and Trust Company.

When the National Banking Act was enacted in 1863 for the establishment of National banks, they were also given authority to issue United States currency. For many years national banks continued to issue this currency which was secured by United States Bonds. We also asked for authority to issue currency, in the amount of $25,000.00. The currency was imprinted with the name Rapid City National Bank, and facsimile signatures of Roy Dean, President, and A. E. Dahl, Cashier, were printed on the currency. We had a redemption fund with the United States Treasurer of $1,250.00, and mutilated currency was charged to it. We then replenished the fund, and additional currency was sent to our bank, which we passed out over the counter like any other currency. The act relating to national bank currency was repealed within a couple of years after we opened for business, and national banks no longer have this privilege. I still have a few pieces of this currency in my safe deposit box, including bill number one.

During the second year our growth continued. We were busy making friends, and deposits drifted our way. Our directors met regularly and they were helpful inasmuch as they had a wider acquaintance and knew more people than I did. We did not always agree, and one of the directors complained I was too conservative. Nearly every day we met for luncheon exchanging ideas for the further promotion of the bank.

The severe drought continued into 1935. There was no feed for the livestock, and prices were at an all-time low. To meet the emergency the federal government purchased cattle regardless of kind and weight for $26.00 each, giving the mortgagee, if the cattle were mortgaged, $16.00 to apply on the debt, and the balance to the borrower. Because the loans we had taken were on such a conservative basis, we sustained no loss on our loans.

When we opened the bank I had about $5,000.00 in cash, and besides my car and household furnishings, that was all. I used $1,750.00 to purchase my fifty shares of stock in the bank. In 1935 we decided to build a home at 615 West Boulevard. The cost was $8,500.00 and I used the balance of my money for a down payment and obtained an FHA loan for $5,000. I was now short of cash, and if I had known the house would cost so much, I would have obtained a larger FHA loan.

Most of the stockholders of the bank were not much interested in bank stock, but purchased the stock to help organize the bank. The result was that many were interested in selling their stock. Realizing this, the directors made an agreement that if any stock was offered for sale, the stock would be put on the table and divided equally. We bought stock as it was offered, but without any cash I was hard put to buy my proportionate share. So I borrowed personally from the directors because it was convenient. I could have borrowed from one of our correspondent banks, which I should have done. I realized my mistake when at the annual meeting the amount of my salary was in question. The directors reminded me how good they had been to lend me money to buy the stock, and I decided then and there that I was not going to be under any obligation to them any more on this score.

Alvin Johnson, president of the Live Stock National Bank of Omaha, one of our correspondent banks, came to call upon us. I had never met Mr. Johnson before, but he became one of my best friends. He was an aggressive banker and was doing a great job at his bank in Omaha. I mentioned to him my debt to the directors, and he asked me how much I owed them. I told him it was not much, and as I remember it was about $2,500.00. He said, "We will fix that. You send a note down to our bank and we will take care of your borrowing needs." I paid my notes to the directors in full.

This became a fine connection and a great help to me. When I had an opportunity to buy bank stock, I would borrow from them, and as I saved money I would pay the notes. The Live Stock National Bank was later merged into the Omaha National Bank. They treated me equally well and have been most helpful. Over the years I have borrowed thousands of dollars from them, and at one time reached a high of about $90,000.00 at the time the Western National Bank was chartered. I owed them various amounts for about twenty-five years, and it was only in recent years that I paid them in full. If it had not been for their help, I would not have been able to accumulate the bank stock I have today. Credit can be a wonderful thing when properly used.

We got into trouble on one loan. When Prohibition was abolished, liquor was sold legally in South Dakota for the first time. In Rapid City three wholesale liquor dealers were licensed, and one of them was our customer. We had a request to loan our customer money on liquor to be stored in a bonded warehouse. Now this was a business about which we knew very little, and even less about all of the off-brand liquor that was flooding the market at the time. The directors decided this was now a legal business and that we could make the loan. Later the company got into trouble, and one morning we were surprised to hear the owners had transferred the stock of the company to a distributor in St. Paul, and the company was out of business. Our loan was then about $5,000.00 and it looked as if we had ample security. We were told we could not foreclose and sell the liquor without a wholesale license costing $3,500.00. This amount would wipe out our equity.

So I sent a telegram to the distributor stating I intended to sell the security under the name and license of our customer. It was not long before the telephone rang. It was the distributor and he said we could not do that. I asked why. He said he did not want his brands of liquor sold in Rapid City below wholesale price. I asked if that was his only objection, and he answered yes. I called on two druggists who had retail liquor licenses. I sold them the brands handled by the distributor at the regular full price, but I sold them other brands for little or nothing, and realized enough to have our loan paid. Later the company filed bankruptcy. We did not lose any money, but we learned a few lessons from this experience.

We also became involved with a loan on postage stamps. The borrower bought every new issue with the intention of holding them until there was a premium on the stamps. He had a large collection when he asked for a loan of $13,000.00, with a margin to spare. Included were some old stamps with a large premium like the unperforated Farleys. Things did not work out as he had planned and the interest was eating up his equity. He could not pay the loan. So we agreed to purchase some of his stamps and use them in the bank on our mailings. Soon the postmaster called on us and wanted to know where we got our stamps. There was nothing wrong, but he explained it hurt his sales.

When the bank examiner came, he wanted to see our collateral. I took him to the basement vault and showed him three large suitcases full of stamps and asked if he wanted to count them. He threw up his hands and said he had never seen so many stamps before. He said he would take our word that we had ample collateral. We also had several large denomination air mail stamps we could not use. I wrote the First National Bank of Minneapolis, and asked if their bank could use the stamps. One of the officers called the postoffice in Minneapolis asking if they would buy the stamps. I could have told him that the postal department will not take back any stamps. The postmaster became suspicious that we had some stolen stamps and sent a postal inspector to call on us. He found the borrower had good title so that ended the visit. Finally we sold most of the stamps to a stamp dealer in Ohio, and the loan was paid in full with interest.

We had no air conditioner in those days and it really got hot in the bank. Roy Dean came to our rescue one day, bringing in a tub of ice and a fan, and we were more comfortable.

The Federal Housing Administration Act became law in 1935. We made the first FHA loan in Rapid City and one of the first in South Dakota. Since then we have made nearly five thousand FHA loans totaling fifty million dollars. We have made more FHA loans than any other bank, savings and loan, mortgage company, or any other lender in South Dakota.

Our staff also grew. In addition to Walter Pailing, we employed Ray Glade as teller, Martin Cobb as bookkeeper, and A. A. Karley as part--time fieldman.

We had a good year in our first full year of operation. Our net earnings, after income taxes, amounted to $12,811.24. We added $1,000.00 to the surplus fund. Dividend on the preferred stock amounted to $1,916.67. We paid our first dividend on the common stock in the amount of $1.00 a share for a total of $2,000.00. We had $8,596.09 left in the undivided profit account.

Our deposits grew from $741,173.21 to $1,229,291.61 during the year.

85

13

Nineteen Thirty Six

At the annual meeting I was promoted to executive vice president and W. E. Shoberg to cashier. Earl Keller and Loren Myli were elected assistant cashiers.

With business increasing we were crowded for room. We built a balcony for our bookkeepers. The steps going up were so steep that it was almost like going up a ladder. We also remodeled the interior of the bank, installing complete new fixtures of the low, friendly type. We provided a larger lobby and more space for my office. We installed new lighting fixtures and provided a new acoustic sound-absorbing ceiling. We purchased a Recordak for microfilming all our checks, one of the first in South Dakota, but used in most banks today.

One of the highlights of the year was purchasing of the assets and assuming the liabilities of the Hermosa State Bank. The bank had survived the hard times, but it was so small in a small town that they could not make any money. They also had losses they

We Started Banking Here

Interior View of Bank

Dean, Swander, Dahl, Devereaux

could not absorb. Herb Brockett, cashier, and two of the principal stockholders called and asked if we would take the bank over. We agreed. It was necessary to have a stockholders' meeting. There were about twenty stockholders in and near Hermosa, and they were called in for a special meeting. It was a surprise to many of them, but it was either a sale of the bank to us or a stockholders' assessment, so they did not have much choice. After the meeting the stockholders went across the street to a restaurant for coffee, and the word soon spread. A few talked about stopping the purchase. The next day was Armistice Day. We decided to act in a hurry, and took all the records to our bank. We announced the purchase and stated that the deposits of the bank were now in the Rapid City National Bank. The total deposits were about $200,000. Although many of the customers were skeptical at first, they liked our bank, and we did not lose any customers. We liquidated the remaining assets and paid the stockholders the amount over the deposit liability. We sustained no loss on the loans. It was a good deal for us.

In our haste to take the bank over, we did not notify either the national banking department or the Federal Deposit Insurance Corporation. Later the FDIC reprimanded us for not obtaining their approval first, but they dropped the matter. I do not remember that the national bank authorities said anything.

The job of a loan officer is not an easy one. I found it nerve-racking and tiresome as I grew older. A banker wants to say "yes," but this is sometimes difficult until he has all the facts. To obtain the facts often takes time, and in the meantime he explores every possibility so he can grant the loan. I learned many years ago not to say "no" until I had all the facts. My first reaction may be negative, but often as I learn more about the applicant, I find things I did not know, and the loan is made.

I remember many years ago a business man came and

asked for a loan of $25,000.00. He was not a customer of the bank and I had heard he was not a good business man. My first reaction was not to make the loan. He furnished me with his financial statements and showed the progress he had made. I was surprised. Perhaps some of the information I had heard was inspired by competitors and others who did not know him and had a personal feeling against him. After thoroughly going through his figures and making some checks as to their accuracy, I concluded he was a reasonably good bank credit risk, and made the loan. He transferred his business to us. He became a good customer, and we never had any trouble with any of his loans. It taught me a lesson not to make hasty decisions when a man or woman asks for a loan.

When I was a bank examiner I often heard bankers talk with their customers, and sometimes I heard things I did not like. I do not think it is as true today, but some bankers talked and acted as though they were doing the borrower a great favor. I do not feel that way. When a man comes to the bank to ask for a loan, I think he is doing the bank a favor, and it is an opportunity to make friends and bring business to the bank. "What do you want the money for?" How many times I have heard that as the first question the banker asks. It depends on the size of the loan, but it should not be the first question. I feel that if the borrower asks for a nominal amount or an amount well within his ability to pay, it is none of the banker's business what the money is for. If it is a large amount, then it becomes a different question and the banker should be entitled to know.

One time many years ago a lady came in and asked for a $1,500.00 loan, which was well within her ability to pay. I did not ask her what she wanted the money for, but quickly wrote out a note which she signed, and credited her account. She heaved a sigh, and said,

"Mary (not her name), let this be a lesson to you."
Curiously, I asked what was wrong. She explained she
had been in Deadwood the night before and had lost
this money gambling.

It has always been the policy of this bank when an
applicant comes in for a loan, particularly if he is a new
one, to place him at ease as soon as possible. I appreciate that an applicant is, so to speak, sitting on a "hot
seat" wondering if he will obtain the loan. I tell my
loan officers to get him off the "hot seat" just as soon as
possible. If you know you are going to make the loan,
tell him so quickly. If you do not know before the interview, thank him for coming in and tell him you are
going to try to make arrangements to grant the loan.
Then the information you need comes easily and quickly. Contrast this with the attitude of the banker who
gives no assuring statement, takes out a financial statement and asks him how much money he has in the bank
and about his accounts receivable and other property.
The borrower still wonders if he will get the loan and
continues to sit on the "hot seat."

I remember an experience several years ago from
which I derived much pleasure and satisfaction. A man,
possibly in his thirties, came in and asked for a loan of
$4,000.00. I knew this man, but he was not a customer.
I knew very little about his financial affairs. I did know
he had a good position, came from a good family, and I
really thought he had more than I found he had. I
learned he had a $9,000.00 salary, equity in his home, a
car, some life insurance, but not much more. He wanted
the $4,000.00 to invest in a small business in connec-
tion with the business he was operating. So I told him
I would make the loan. He asked what security I wanted and I said "none," which surprised him. He was
very appreciative. Later I learned from another source
that he had applied for the loan at another bank, and
they wanted security on everything he had. He was

having coffee at the A & F Cafe with one of our customers, and when he complained about what the other bank wanted, my customer said to him, "Why don't you go and see Art Dahl." That is how he came to us. The reason I did not ask for security was that this man had substantial income and there was no question about his ability to pay the loan, and any security we could have had would be equities. I felt it did not add anything to the paper, because we were lending largely on his income and ability to pay. He paid the bank as agreed, made himself some money, and became a valued customer. He sent us other business and became one of the best boosters for this bank. He told one of his associates how well he was treated, and he came in and opened a $2,000.00 account. It is the way you treat your customers that counts, and I am sure our growth has been due in large part to knowing how to make loans and take reasonable bank risks. If you treat one customer well, he sends more business to the bank.

We had another profitable year. We added $4,000.-00 to the surplus fund and retired $2,875.00 of preferred stock. We also paid a dividend of $2,115.00 to the common stockholders. Our deposits increased to $1,873,-921.73, a substantial amount for the year.

14

Nineteen Thirty Seven

Since the day our bank opened, we have continued a consistent advertising program. Most banks, including our competition, did very little advertising in those days. Most banks seemed to have a feeling that advertising was below their dignity. Perhaps many did not know how to advertise, or were so busy making loans that they did not have the time. Maybe we were a little out of step in spending so much money for advertising, but it must have done us a lot of good. One unkind person said the Rapid City National Bank bragged too much. Whether it was an inspired statement, I do not know and I did not care. I find the automobile manufacturers, cigarette companies and other large companies do not hesitate to tell the world they have the best car or the best cigarette. If you do not tell the public and your customers about yourself, who will?

When you advertise you have a twofold purpose: First, to attract new business, and second, to keep your customers informed. Your satisfied customers like to say nice things about you, but you must also furnish them facts about your institution so they know what to say.

I have always had an interest in advertising. In Toronto and in Castlewood I mimeographed a monthly letter to our customers. In Rapid City I felt we had a better medium in the newspapers and on radio. Advertising, to be successful, must be planned and consistent. Spasmodic advertising with Christmas and holiday greetings has little value. Also much of the canned advertising you may purchase, in my opinion, has little value because it does not reflect your bank.

From the time of our organization more than thirty-one years ago, we have never failed to have an advertisement in the Rapid City Daily Journal each week. Since radio station KOTA commenced business about twenty-five years ago, we have sponsored the seven o'-clock morning newscast. These two mediums have been our mainstay year after year, and I am sure this advertising has had much to do with our growth. We also use other newspapers and radio stations.

We have tried to write our own advertising in plain, everyday language — just the way we talk to people. They may not be artistic and perhaps not always grammatically correct, but they are representative of our bank and its people. We have tried to avoid such trite expressions as "complete banking services" and "friendly bank." If you have a friendly bank the people will know it and it seems foolish to label yourself a "friendly bank." The service you perform and the way you treat people will speak for themselves. I think most people look upon us as a friendly bank, but that is their opinion.

I realize the percentage of people who will read all of a bank advertisement is comparatively small. For that reason I have always tried to say as much as possible in the title of the advertisement, since a greater number of people will read the headline. You can often say much in a few words.

If you have a good advertisement that pulls, there is nothing wrong in repeating it at a later time. The audience changes with newcomers coming to town, and the old residents may have missed it the first time. If I see a good advertisement of another bank, I file it away, and at a later time I use the idea, changing it to fit this bank and community.

Whenever there is a call for a report on the condition of the bank, we take advantage of the opportunity to run a large three-quarter-page advertisement in the local paper. It is important, we feel, to accompany our statement with narrative facts, calling attention to some feature of the statement, telling of our progress, or saying something about our bank that may be of interest to the readers. Many people will look at the figures casually and not understand their significance, but they will read narrative facts and understand them.

At the year end we take a full page and feature the "Highlights of the Year." We also show our comparative growth, and at this time we usually have room for our officers and directors. We tell our community more about our bank than most banks do, and they like it. Furthermore, many people may not give the advertisement more than a casual glance, but they gain a favorable impression from the fact that the bank must be strong and doing well, otherwise the bank would not publish their statement so completely.

In reading the year-end advertisements of banks in the American Banker, I find that a large number of banks take as much space as the statement to feature their directors and affiliations. I am sure the listing of the directors so prominently flatters the ego of the directors, but I doubt it has much pulling power to bring in business. I have noticed, however, an advertisement of a large New York bank featuring narrative facts about

"Money at Work," which was very good, but this bank is an exception. At times we do list our directors, but they will not occupy a very large space.

Annually we have prepared our report in booklet form and mailed it to customers, stockholders, and friends. We have given customers more information about the bank than has any other bank in this area. The report includes vital information in pictures, figures, and narrative facts. We feel this policy of giving our customers this information has been an important factor in our growth.

We have mailed out in the latter years 15,000 reports annually. This has been a big undertaking in January of each year, and the postage adds up to a considerable amount. In 1964 we had a new idea. We printed the annual report as a supplement to the Rapid City Daily Journal at a considerable saving in both work and money. Since this paper has a circulation of more than 30,000 subscribers, we were able to place our report in twice as many homes as previously. We received many favorable comments.

The supplement report is colorful. On the front page this year we have a picture of our officers and staff in the main bank lobby. We also have pictures of the people working in all our branches. Other features include: Highlights of 1964; a message over the signature of Mr. Pailing and myself; names of officers and employees identifying them on the pictures; pictures of our bank buildings and interior lobby; statement of condition; our growth in chart and figures; a list showing investments in bonds and classification of loans in considerable detail; a breakdown of deposits; features about our Auto Bank; news about our trust department and travel department; something about the mural; a brief history of the bank; and on the back page a picture of our directors with their names, concluding with a list of our officers. It is written so the man on the street can understand it, with pictures which often tell more than words. The report is a sales medium advertising our bank and its services.

Some banks hire an advertising agency, and there are some very good ones, but the banker then leaves it to the agency to handle all the advertising. I don't think it is entirely successful. Agencies do not know your business as you do. They cannot reflect the personality of your bank and know what to say. It may work if one of the top officers takes an interest in the advertisements and works with the agency.

I have personally written most of the advertisements for our bank. After all, I think the top officer is the sales manager of the bank, and his prime duty is to bring business to the bank. I do not find it particularly difficult, and often pound out an advertisement on my typewriter quite quickly, writing in my own words the thoughts as they come to me, almost like writing a letter to a friend.

While I am on this subject of advertising, I may as well say something about give-aways. I do not believe in give-aways. The wrong people often receive the gifts, and there are professionals who go from one business to another to see what they can have for nothing. The best customers are often missed. I think people do business with our bank because we give them what they want in the best banking service, and not because we give them pencils, pocketbooks, matches, and many other things. Not long ago one of my competitors gave away Easter bonnets, and another gave Gold Bond stamps. A lady asked one of our officers what we gave away. He answered, "Nothing, except the best banking service in town." In our thirty-one years we have never given match books with our name on them. I question whether we would have one more dollar on deposits if we had provided matches for our customers and friends. I do know we have saved thousands of dollars, and I am in the banking business to make money, and not to give it away. The last salesman for a match company, after our refusal, said: "What reason am I going to give the boss this time for not being able to sell you matches?" I told him to tell the boss I was the toughest banker he had met. He answered he could not do that because another South Dakota banker was tougher — he had kicked him out of the bank.

Calendars were the principal give-aways and the most common form of advertising for banks when I started in the banking business. We had big calendars for the business firms and small calendars for homes. We were no exception when we opened the Rapid City National Bank, and we had calendars, both big and small. One day many years ago while I was standing in the lobby, a lady with an armful of calendars came in and asked for a calendar. I asked where she lived and she replied by naming a town east of here, outside our normal banking area. It was the old story — our own customers most entitled to a calendar did not receive one nor did they want one, but we were furnishing calendars to many who did not bank with us or never would. We decided calendars brought us little, if any, business and we discontinued them. I do not think we lost any business. Later we did substitute a small celluloid calendar which we purchased in sufficient quantities to enclose one in each of the monthly statements to all our customers. They have proved popular. Since the cost and size are comparatively small, we can distribute them to all our customers.

I am a strong believer in advertising, but it has to be done with a planned purpose, with much thought and preparation and with sincere frankness, telling the public about the bank and its services. Some of the advertising I have seen is just a waste of money. You must be enthusiastic about your bank. We may have been the biggest braggart in town, but it has brought us business.

Advertising is like putting seed in the ground. Some seeds grow and others do not, but a consistent policy of seeding can be of great help in making a bank grow.

We had a profitable year and added $15,000.00 to the Surplus Fund and paid our third annual dividend of $1.00 a share. The deposits grew more slowly, but we ended the year with a new high in deposits totaling $1,924,784.94.

15

Nineteen Thirty Eight

Carl E. Behrens resigned as director. He had not wanted to be a director in the first place and had accepted the position only because we had difficulties finding directors when we opened for business. W. E. Shoberg was elected to replace him on the board.

The directors decided they wanted to be paid $100.-00 a month for their directorships. I personally did not object, because the bank was now earning money and the directors did spend a lot of time, perhaps much more than most directors. The amount was much larger, however, than the amount paid directors in other banks. I found that the directors wanted to be well paid themselves, but when it came to my salary, before, then and afterwards, they were reluctant to grant a raise. Never in the history of the bank have the directors come to me and said: "Art, you have done a good job so we will raise your salary next year." I have no complaint now since the officers of this bank, including myself, are among the best paid in the industry.

Everything was fine until Walter Olson, national bank examiner, came. He hit the ceiling and said they do not pay that much in directors' fees at the First National Bank of St. Paul. I told him it was not my idea and he could take it up with the directors. It was decided we would have a directors' meeting with the examiner at seven o'clock in the evening. I was to leave on the train later that evening. Mr. Olson stated his views and I remember Mr. Swander took a good look at him and said: "Well, if this directorship is a one-way street, with much liability and no compensation, I will offer my resignation as a director." Swander had been on the depositors' committee of the closed Pennington County Bank, and had had a part in collecting the directors' liability of that bank. That took the wind out of Mr. Olson, and after some discussion, he decided to drop the matter. We have continued to pay our non-officer directors $100 a month and have until this day. I guess Mr. Olson felt a little bad about the way he had roughed me up, and he told Shoberg to tell me, upon my return, that he was making no criticisms and that in his confidential report to the Comptroller of Currency he rated our bank in the top bracket.

We continued to gain on our competition in deposits, and on September 28, 1938, the last official statement published before their consolidation, the comparative deposits were as follows:

Rapid City National Bank $2,090,630.28

First National Bank of Rapid City $2,425,916.36

The First National Bank on October 1, 1938, was consolidated with the banks in Lead, Deadwood, Belle Fourche, Newell, Hot Springs, Spearfish and Sturgis, and became a nine million dollar bank distributed in eight banking offices against our one office in Rapid City. It was perhaps not long after this time that we passed them in Rapid City deposits, a lead we have maintained since, and in substantial amount in the latter years.

Robert H. Driscoll moved to Rapid City to become president of the First National Bank of the Black Hills, and he became a formidable competitor. I know that during the time he was managing officer we had the toughest competition. The name Driscoll was a big name in banking in the Black Hills. His father had been a distinguished and very successful banker for many years in the Black Hills. Bob also had prestige which brought business to the bank. Bob and I became warm friends, a friendship I have always valued highly. He now lives in California, but he always comes to the bank for a visit on his trips to Rapid City.

We closed the year with deposits of $2,221,334.59.

16

Nineteen Thirty Nine

The bank was now nearly five years old and we had done very well. Looking back, I feel that one reason for our success was that we created a favorable image of the kind of bank we were from the very start. We were very conservative and people looked upon us as a sound bank. I think it is of the greatest importance for a new bank to first build a favorable image so that the people of the community have confidence in the bank. The bank and its officers must build the respect of the community.

In the first year we saw the need of having good information about our customers so we could serve them well and quickly. We established a most complete central information file. Many banks have central information files, but our file is more complete than any I have seen in any other bank anywhere, and we know it has been most helpful in giving our customers better service.

Here is a photocopy of the card.

The card is eight by five inches and is stored in a rotary cabinet with room for about twenty-five thousand

Central File Card

Yr	Dp	Ln		YEAR 1958 Aver. Bal.	Loan	YEAR 1959 Aver. Bal.	Loan	YEAR 1960 Aver. Bal.	Loan	YEAR 1961 Aver. Bal.	Loan	YEAR 1962 Aver. Bal.	Loan	YEAR 1963 Aver. Bal.	Loan
34			Jan.												
35			Feb.												
36			Mar.												
37			April												
38			May												
39			June												
40			July												
41			Aug.												
42			Sept.												
43			Oct.												
44			Nov.												
45			Dec.												

				YEAR 1964		YEAR 1965		YEAR 1966		YEAR 1967		YEAR 1968		YEAR 1969	
46			Jan.												
47			Feb.												
48			Mar.												
49			April												
50			May												
51			June												
52			July												
53			Aug.												
54			Sept.												
55			Oct.												
56			Nov.												
57			Dec.												

Front

ACCOUNT OPENED

Kind	Date	Amount

RESIDENCE

PREVIOUS RESIDENCE

PREVIOUS BANK

OCCUPATION

PERSONAL HISTORY

REMARKS:

Back of Card

cards. It covers a period of twelve years. We are now on the third set, and if a customer had an account in prior years, it is noted on the left. At the end of the month each card is posted. Under average balance we show in black ink the balance in the checking account, with red ink the balance in the savings account, and if our customer has a savings certificate it is posted in green ink. In the next column under loans we show in black ink the amount owing in our commercial department, in red ink the installment loans, and if the customer has a mortgage, it is shown in green ink. Presently we do not average any more, but post the amount of the deposit and loan at the end of the month.

On the reverse side of the card we have information as to when the account was opened, previous residence of the customer and also previous bank. There is a place for occupation, personal history when available, and further remarks. This card is made up when the account is opened, and we obtain as much information about our customer as possible without being nosy.

Here is how it works. One of our customers approaches one of our loan officers for a loan, say a couple of hundred dollars. If he is not known to the officer, the officer asks his name and goes to the central information file for his card. He can see at a glance the kind of account the customer has, whether he has borrowed before. In this case, let us assume he has not borrowed before, but has had an account with us a few years, with a moderate balance, and the position he holds indicates he has the income to pay the loan requested. He receives the loan quickly, and he leaves with praise for the prompt service he has received.

Now suppose a bank does not have such a complete central file. The banker will ask him if he has an account or if he has borrowed here before — all this information I always thought a banker should have about a customer.

On the other hand, if the card shows a very small balance, and there have been overdrafts, the information will be available. If we have had previous unsatisfactory experience with the applicant, the information will be on the back of the card. He cannot have an unsatisfactory experience with one officer, who may be absent that day, and then try to obtain a loan from another officer, because the record will be shown on the card.

We do not run a credit check on all new accounts opened. If we have to run a credit check later with the local credit bureau, the information is noted on the card and preserved. It saves time for the officers to make a duplicate credit check later. If we receive a recommendation from another bank where the customer has previously banked, this is summarized on the card. The central file is also helpful to cross-check against other accounts carried by the customer, the accounts carried by the wife or husband or other affiliated accounts.

Overdrafts are always a headache to a banker. Every day we check new overdrafts against our central information card. If this is the first time the customer overdraws his account, the card indicates he has carried a satisfactory account before, chances are we will pay the check. If we also notice the customer has a balance in his savings account, we pay the overdraft. Then if we return a check, we note in pencil in the proper month "ret," which means we have returned a check, and if there are previously returned checks, we do not make the mistake of paying the overdraft because of lack of information.

I can hear bankers say: "But it is expensive to keep such complete information, and it takes lots of work." Sure, it takes both work and money, but this is more than offset because we make fewer mistakes, fewer bad loans, have fewer bad overdrafts, and the cost of clerical help is more than offset by the time saved by the officers. I am confident we have more readily available information about our customers and we have been able to serve them better and more quickly. The central information file has more than paid for itself by satisfied customers who like the way we do business. I cannot estimate the amount of additional business or how much it has added to our growth, but I am sure it is very substantial.

At this time we were crowded for room and tried to purchase the adjoining property, but we could not make a deal. This was fortunate and we made plans to find another location.

Our staff had grown to sixteen active officers and employees. From the annual report I note we had 2,847 checking accounts, 1,125 savings accounts, 145 time certificates, 2,365 loans, and 516 safe deposit box accounts, for a total of 6,998 accounts. This compares with 6,001 accounts the previous year.

The deposits at the year end were $2,573,489.82.

17

Nineteen Forty

As we entered upon the year 1940, the directors decided to revamp our capital structure, which was approved by the stockholders at the annual meeting. The plan provided that we should sell $100,000.00 in preferred stock to local investors. We would increase our common stock from $55,000.00 to $100,000.00 by a transfer of $45,000.00 from the undivided profit account. The preferred stock held by the Reconstruction Finance Corporation would be paid in full. The new stock carried a five per cent dividend, and we had no trouble selling the $100,000.00 preferred stock to people in the community.

The quick acceptance and purchase of the preferred stock showed that people again had confidence in the banking business and, in particular, they had confidence in the Rapid City National Bank. Contrast this with the year 1934 when we opened for business; it was difficult to sell any bank stock for cash.

In November Edward H. Swander, director, died

suddenly. He attended a meeting at the bank in the morning and before noon he was dead. Mr. Swander took the directorship for only one year when we opened for business, but he soon found he enjoyed his directorship, and he never again mentioned resigning. I am sure the six and one-half years he was a director was one of the highlights of his life, and at times he seemed to take greater interest in the bank than in his bakery business. He contributed much to the bank and was one of the best boosters I had. He was a sound and progressive business man and an enthusiastic booster for the community. He had a high sense of honor and loyalty.

Earl Keller, assistant cashier, was elected director to fill the vacancy on the board.

Our deposits had now grown to $2,892,944.02.

18

Nineteen Forty One

With the growth of the bank our banking quarters became too small. Thoughtful consideration was given to further remodeling, obtaining additional room in adjoining buildings or leasing other quarters, but these plans were abandoned in favor of a new building. Now we had the problem of finding a site. Otto Kepp owned the corner of St. Joe and Seventh Streets and he offered us the site for $30,000.00. I was willing and recommended the purchase, but the directors did not agree, but said it was too much, and the matter drifted along for a month. One day I again visited Otto Kepp and asked if he would consider less so I could sell the plan to the directors. He offered to take $28,000.00 and the directors agreed. I was very sorry we asked Otto to take a cut in his price. We paid him plenty when we bought from him the remaining two lots nearly twenty years later.

We employed A. Moorman & Company of Minneapolis, specialists in bank architecture, and one of the oldest such firms in the Northwest. The new building

Bank Christmas Party 1938

Shoberg, Devereaux, Dean, Dahl, Keller

Our First Home in Rapid City

would be two stories with basement 140 by 50 feet. The contract was let in October, and war was declared one month later. We were fearful we would not be able to obtain material, but we placed our orders immediately and the building was completed on time.

I quote from our annual report: "You have seen our crowded bank lobby. You have seen our officers and employees crowded into every available space on the main floor, balcony, and basement. You have seen the large number of checks drawn on this bank. You have liked the many new banking services we introduced making this bank useful to a greater number of people. And now, with the establishment of the air base here, it means even more people and more customers."

At the time I commenced my banking experience in 1917 there were no such things as service charges. We took all accounts offered to us regardless of balance, and a large portion of our accounts were carried at a continuous loss. To offset this loss the banks had to charge more interest to their borrowers. Many of our borrowers in those days paid us ten per cent interest on their loans. The deposits in the small accounts contributed little if anything in the way of loanable funds. It was a very unfair situation, having some of the customers paying the losses created by other customers. Perhaps many banks would have survived the depression days if they had had realistic service charges.

Later banks began having service fees by charging the small accounts fifty cents per month when their balance dropped below one hundred dollars. Although this may have been better than no service charge, it was not the answer. Many large activity accounts were carried at a loss. Most banks now base their service charges on activity with a credit for the balance carried. The larger accounts may not pay any service charges, but the small accounts and the large activity accounts will pay a reasonable price for the cost of handling the accounts.

With the measured service charge plan, the size of the accounts does not make much difference. We have been able to invite everybody's accounts, whether large, small, or in between. If the balance is insufficient to pay the costs, the customer pays for the service. No bank today can operate without reasonable service fees. Today service charges contribute substantially to the earnings of a good bank.

Sometimes we read or hear about new banks opening for business offering to take accounts without service charges or they pay more interest than established banks. This I do not believe to be a good policy. When we opened this bank, we learned what charges were made by our competitor, and we adopted their schedule. I feel the problem of a new bank is to build the image that it is a strong and sound bank and that the management is careful and competent. I do not think a bank can build this image by giving free service on checking accounts, upsetting the established rate on savings in the community, spending large amounts of money for elaborate quarters they will not need for a long time to come, which results in a big loss in operating earnings and depletion of the capital funds paid in.

The necessity of service charges in a bank was forcefully demonstrated in Tulsa, Oklahoma, where a new bank promised no service fee for life to the people opening accounts in the new bank. People came by the thousands: parents opened accounts for all their children, babies and all, with nominal amounts, so they would have no service charges when they grew up, and for life. The press stated that they received 30,000 accounts. The bank had to purchase equipment to handle the accounts, and they hired a large number of new people in a hurry, without the necessary experience. The result was so much confusion and mess that they could not properly handle the accounts. Deposits were posted to the wrong accounts, checks were paid where there were insufficient funds on deposit, and the overdraft account grew large. It became an impossible situation, making it necessary for the Comptroller of Currency to appoint a conservator, and the bank was succeeded by another new bank, which was not bound by the agreement to provide free checking account services. The bank was capitalized for about $900,000.00 and a recent news dispatch in the American Banker said stockholders would lose $600,-000.00, or two-thirds of their investment. The depositors did not lose anything, but a great many of them closed their accounts in the succeeding bank when there was no more free service. How stupid can bankers be to saddle their bank with no service charge for life? It is a lesson that bankers should observe.

This bank has always had service charges and they are an important part of our income. Our service charges are simple. We have a basic charge of 60 cents per account, plus six cents for each check and deposit. We credit fifteen cents for each one hundred dollars average balance carried by the customers. Where the balance is sufficient to carry the activity, there will be no charge. We discontinued making a charge for collection of out-of-town items.

We retired $50,000.00 of the preferred stock we had sold nearly two years ago. Our earnings were very good and we are building capital accounts through retained earnings. Our dividend policy has been conservative. The deposits again increased, reaching a new high of $3,194,119.57.

19

Nineteen Forty Two

The year 1942 was one of great activity around Rapid City. The Air Force Base was being constructed east of town. Four of our employees, Walter Pailing, Fred Barth, Ray Glade, and John Brownlee, were serving in the Armed Forces. We sold War Bonds. We had twenty-four officers and employees. Our deposits grew fast.

We moved into the new building over Memorial Day. We had so much room that I thought perhaps we had built too large a building, but not for long. The building and lot represented an investment of $151,000.-00, an amount equal to our common stock, not including surplus and undivided profits. A few bankers took a poke at us for investing our entire capital in brick and mortar, but we had the last laugh. The office space was rented quickly and we had seventeen tenants. With the addition of the rental income, our occupancy expense was low, and the building turned out to be one of the best investments we have made.

The only frills around the building were two solid

Our New Building

Interior View

glass doors that opened electrically when the customer stepped on a rubber mat. We named them our friendly doors. In our advertising we used the slogan: "The friendly doors of the Rapid City National Bank always swing wide for you." They worked well for many years and, since they were the only doors of their kind in Rapid City, they attracted much attention.

We inaugurated a new service for our customers. We opened an After Hours Department in a room at the head of the stairway on the second floor. This department was open from three to five-thirty in the afternoon for customers to make deposits, cash checks, and make loan payments. This service was well received, and was the first extension of banking hours in town.

War inflation was on and our deposits nearly doubled, going from $3,194,246.65 to $6,126,356.70 during the year. The loans dropped $272,664.67, due perhaps to the fact there was a scarcity of goods.

20

Nineteen Forty Three

A highlight of the year was the marriage of our daughter Verley to Harris Torgerson. They became acquainted when Verley was called upon to play the piano accompaniment for Harris and his brother Marlowe when they sang solos and duets, in which they both excelled. Harris later enlisted in the United States Navy as a flier and saw considerable combat service during the war.

One day we received a telegram that he was back in San Francisco and would call in the evening. Gathered at our home were his parents, my wife and I, and of course Verley. He talked at length with all of us. I did not quite understand from my conversation with him that he wanted Verley to come to San Francisco and marry him. I was soon told that this was the plan. Verley left for San Francisco, accompanied by her mother and Mrs. Torgerson, who went along to attend the wedding. Why I did not go I am at a loss to explain, as there was no reason I could not go. I guess I thought it would be just an informal wedding, but afterwards I found they had a big wedding at the Chapel on Treasure Island with all the trimmings. I have always kicked myself for not attending the wedding, but I was very happy her mother was able to go.

They did come home in December, three months later, which was a most enjoyable visit. Harris was again sent to sea for more war duty, and Verley worked at Long Beach during his absence. He received the Distinguished Flying Cross for his service.

The year 1943 brought us further growth with substantial increase in deposits. The loans remained about the same. We had seven employees in the armed forces, and except for the three active officers, our staff was all girls.

It was now nearly ten years since the bank opened. The records of the bank showed we had made 37,023 loans for a total of $17,675,012.13, not including any renewals. The net losses in this ten-year period were $7,936.91.

We closed the year with $7,299,190.97 in deposits.

21

Nineteen Forty Four

Up to now Roy Dean had been president and I was executive vice president. Walking down the street to attend Rotary Club, I asked Roy if he would be chairman and let me be president. "Fine," Roy replied. When the word spread, one of the other directors came into my office and said he did not approve. This was disheartening since it had been my lifelong ambition to be president. Ten years had elapsed since the bank opened and I had worked hard. Hours meant nothing and I had spent many evenings at the bank working. The directors, however, made the promotion, and I was president.

With the fast growth of the past two years, with deposits nearly three times the deposits we had when we moved into the new building, we were having trouble with the national banking department for inadequate capital. We agreed we were under-capitalized; however, we were determined not to sell any more capital stock unless we were forced to do so, but to increase our capital funds from earnings and limiting the amount of dividends paid.

Mr. Beatty, who was then chief national bank examiner in Minneapolis, wrote me a rather sharp letter stating he wanted to see me in Minneapolis. In those days I took the train to Minneapolis. I had never meet Mr. Beatty. He was very courteous but firm in demanding that we sell $100,000.00 more in common stock, and retire the $50,000.00 preferred stock, which would result in increasing our capital $50,0000.00. I was also firm in maintaining that the earnings would supply the necessary capital and that all we wanted was time. When I left I agreed we would sell $50,000.00 more in common stock and retire the preferred stock but that was all. We seemed to understand each other, and he was always my good friend after that. He agreed that we had a sound bank, and this was possibly the reason he did not press us further for the additional capital.

We offered the stockholders the right to purchase a half share for each share they then owned at $25.00 per share, which was the par value, and without any premium. Our stockholders all subscribed for their share, thereby increasing our common capital to $150,000.00, and total capital accounts to $383,733.04. With deposits over eight million dollars, our ratio of capital to deposits was less than five per cent. Today we have nearly ten per cent capital to deposits. The amount of capital was not so important when the bank was as sound and liquid as the Rapid City National Bank.

I have always considered myself a good credit man and a good collector. I have always been willing to take a credit risk, particularly with men who had character and earning capacity. I have been out on the limb many times, but I have had the ability to smell a bad deal, probably a little faster than many bankers, call a halt, and if necessary, be tough and collect the money before it developed into a loss. Mr. Wray, the national bank examiner mentioned earlier, told me one day after an examination that he did not classify many loans he would ordinarily classify if the same loans were found in another bank, for he felt they did not have the same risk in our bank because we had a strong collection policy and a record of good collections.

I have had some interesting experiences in making loans. A long time ago a borrower presented a statement asking for a loan. I looked over the statement and with some checking found he had all the assets shown, but he had forgotten to list all his liabilities. I guess I lost my temper. I threw the statement at him and told him not to bring any more "funny" statements if he expected me to loan him money. We continued to be good friends and I loaned this man money after we understood each other, and he was then fair and honest with me. Another man gave me a statement and asked if there was any chance anyone else would see the statement. I asked him why he was so concerned, and I finally found it was different from the one he gave the Internal Revenue Department. I returned his statement and told him the only credit he could have from this bank in the future was the statement he submitted to the government. We got along pretty well after that.

It is always a great satisfaction to make loans to help people grow and prosper. Many of the prominent people in Rapid City were small borrowers with small means in the earlier days of our bank. We extended credit to many of them and it was profitable for them and for our bank. One of the most substantial men in Rapid City today started with us many years ago in our installment loan department.

Among the many who have been most successful was a young man who came into the bank just after graduation from high school and asked to borrow $500.00 to start a snake garden. I was taken by surprise, but before I could say anything, he said his father would sign the note with him. He received the loan. That young man was Earl Brockelsby, who has given me permission to tell this story. Today he has one of the largest lines of credit in this bank. Our faith in a young man nearly thirty years ago has been a rewarding satisfaction to us both. I could mention many more.

I feel our bank has had a reasonably liberal loan policy, and our growth would not have been possible if we had not been willing to take an ordinary bank credit risk. I particularly like to make loans to young men who are energetic and know how to handle money. I always look to the income of the borrower. I am not so much concerned with his financial statement — which may not always be so strong — as with the borrower's ability to make money. I learned long ago that it takes income to pay debts. Property will not pay debts without putting a man out of business.

Our deposits at the year end were $8,138,035.65.

22

Nineteen Forty Five

The year 1945 brought sorrow to our family. My wife Lillie, to whom I had been married for twenty-three years, passed away on January 5. She died of sarcoma cancer after a long illness. She had been a loyal, faithful wife, helpful and considerate, and I owe much to her for my success.

During the ten years and nine months since the bank opened, I had worked hard days and nights, often to the neglect of my family. We were thrifty and spent little for entertainment and amusement, but saved every penny so I could continue to purchase and increase my investment in the bank. We had a nice home which she loved. She passed away at about the time we had reached our goal financially and we could have enjoyed the fruits of our hard work and thrift.

I was having coffee one morning with the late Dr. E. W. Minty. In the course of the conversation he made the remark: "Many young men fail because they do not want to pay the price of success when they are young."

What he meant was that many young men and women spend all they earn and save nothing to take advantage of the opportunity when it comes. I have always believed every family should save at least a part of their income, even though it may be a small amount.

Whether I am a good example or not I do not know, but I do think there were many young men who were as thrifty and careful with money as I was in that ten-year period. I had a goal and I succeeded in buying my share of the bank stock I was entitled to.

My debts at this time were nominal, and I had succeeded in buying a sufficient amount of bank stock so I owned about twenty per cent of the outstanding stock, with Roy Dean and Harry Devereaux owning like amounts.

Verley came home about a month before her mother passed away, and Harris was somewhere out in the Pacific flying from a carrier. It was good to have Verley with me for the next nine months until Harris returned, and we continued to live in our home. In fact, it was Verley's home, since we gave it to her by deed before Lillie passed away. It pleased her very much to know Verley would have the home.

On May 2 my grandson Richard was born at the local hospital. It was about three o'clock in the morning, and I was walking the hallway waiting for him to announce his arrival by crying. He did not cry and I became worried, but when the nurse appeared I was assured everything was all right. The next morning I was able to take his picture, but it was a month later before Harris received it and knew he was a father. It was not until five months later that he could return to see his son. Richard is now a junior at Redlands University in California.

Later, after Verley and her family had left, I moved into an apartment at the Alex Johnson Hotel. I also bought a small summer cabin out in the Canyon to putter around with. Life continued on.

The war ended in April. Fred Barth was the first to return. He was elected assistant cashier. Frances Vincent was also elected assistant cashier. W. E. Shoberg was promoted to vice president and Earl Keller became cashier.

This year we made our first G.I. Loan to Mr. and Mrs. Leo Schneider. It was also the first G.I. Loan made in Rapid City with publicity in the newspapers. I think the G.I. program was one of the most successful ever instituted. It was very useful to many ex-service men, and also the home-building field.

As I write this and look over the statements of the bank the past ten years, it seems we always had much more cash on hand than our requirements. I wonder a little why we did not have a larger amount invested. Perhaps it was because I am by nature conservative and also I had been told if we have plenty of money on hand we can always do business. It seems now we could have increased our earnings by investing more of our cash.

Our family have since coming to Rapid City been members of Trinity Lutheran Church. The church was a frame building on the corner of St. Joe and Fourth Streets, and very small for the needs of the church. Some years past I was asked to serve on the building committee. The church had a debt of $2,800.00 and we wanted to purchase a site directly south on Kansas City for $7,000.00. We made up two small charts divided into squares, one for the church debt and one for the purchase of the lots. We worked hard to sell the squares for $25.00 each and succeeded in liquidating the debt and also paying for the new lots. Then we continued to solicit money for the new building. When the war was over we asked for bids on the building. The bids were far above the money available, and many members of the church thought we should postpone building. I disagreed. I told the committee that if we did not decide to build now, it would be a long time before we could build. I further stated that now the war was over, we would very likely have some inflation with higher costs later, and we had better let the contract at once. We did, and as predicted we were able to build a very fine church for less money than if we had waited. We continued to solicit funds, and with a mortgage we were able to pay for the church.

My wife having passed away before the completion of the church, I gave the church a large Moller organ, which could not be replaced today for less than twenty-five thousand dollars. The organ serves as the Dahl Memorial Organ. My daughter Verley was the church organist for many years before leaving Rapid City. I have never missed any money I have donated to my church, and I feel the blessings received have been manifold.

The stockholders had paid in $70,000.00 on the opening day and $50,000.00 in 1944 for a total of $120,000.00. The capital funds were now $412,771.51, a gain of $290,-771.51. In addition, the stockholders had received $91,-615.00 in cash dividends. The success of the bank both in growth of deposits and earnings had been phenomenally good, but I believe it was the strong foundation on which we were building the bank, plus the confidence the bank held in the community, that was the forerunner of greater things to come.

We passed the ten million dollar amount in deposits, ending the year with deposits of $10,757,512.39.

126

23

Nineteen Forty Six

In the year 1946 the postwar boom was in full swing. We were making FHA and GI loans in greater volume. Walter Pailing and Ray Glade returned from the war and were made assistant cashiers.

We paid a fifty thousand stock dividend, giving our stockholders one additional share for each three they owned, increasing our capital stock to two hundred thousand dollars.

As a sidelight, it was in this year that one of our book-keepers made a very large error that could have cost us several thousand dollars, but fortunately we recovered all our money. It was on February 28, the last day of the month. We had two accounts, the Nebraksa Investment Company and the Nebraska Improvement Company. (These two names are fictitious, but the similarity in names is the same.) The Nebraska Improvement Company account was an in-and-out account and more or less inactive when on the books. On that day they made a deposit of $30,000.00, and the bookkeeper, in the rush of the end-of-the-month activity, erroneously credited the deposit to the Nebraska Investment Company. We single-posted, and the bookkeepers had orders to read back the deposits to see if they had been properly posted to the correct account, but failed to do so.

The owner of the Nebraska Investment Company received the statement showing a balance of $30,000.00. He soon commenced writing checks and before the error was discovered he had checked out $13,000.00. Harry Devereaux and I drove to the Nebraska Investment Company and met the owner in the yard of his home. We told him that he had taken money unlawfully and we were here to get it back. He answered we had a notice on our statement which read: "If no error is reported within ten days, the account will be considered correct." That was a new one. Since we had not notified him in ten days he considered the money his. We quickly informed him it did not absolve him for taking money which did not belong to him. He replied he was worth the amount. We wanted to know how soon we could have our money back, and after considerable talk, we adjourned to the kitchen table and obtained a second mortgage on the ranch land and on some trucks and automobiles, payable at $1,000.00 a month. He made the payments for a few months and then refinanced his land mortgage and we were paid in full.

I did not say anything to the bookkeeper who had made the error the first day, but I knew how bad she felt. On the second day I told her not to worry too much. After all it was an honest error, but I added: "Next time please do not make the error so big." The day I received the final payment, she walked past my desk, and I told her she was the only bookkeeper who had made a loan in the bank, and we collected $400.00 interest, but it was not funny to her. She continued to work for us and did a good job.

Banks do make errors, but when you consider the

thousands of deposits and checks handled every day, it is almost amazing that the errors are so few and far between.

When the bank makes an error we quickly correct it to the satisfaction of the customer even though it may cost us money. One morning when I was on the way to the bank, a man stopped me and said he was going to sue the bank. I asked him what was wrong. He said we had charged some of his wife's checks to his account, and she had no authority to write checks. I explained that if we were wrong, he did not have to sue the bank. We found we were in error and credited his account with the total of the checks his wife had written. Subsequently, in a divorce proceeding, the judge ordered him to make good his wife's checks, so we received our money.

On another occasion we made an error crediting $1,000.00 to the wrong account. The deposit should have been credited to the account of a man living in Custer, but by mistake the deposit was credited to a local man with a very similar name. The Custer account was relatively dormant and it was not discovered for a year. The local man who received the deposit never checked it out, and although he received his statement every month, he never came in and told us he had the deposit.

The largest mistake in figures we have made did not involve a customer, but was reporting the total debits to the Federal Reserve Bank. Each month we report to the bank the total debits for Rapid City with comparisons for the previous year, as an indicator of business activity in the community. One of our girls, in adding up the total checks drawn for the month, made a mistake of more than two million dollars, and the report was sent to the bank and published before it was discovered. I called her into my office and we mutually agreed that she was not doing well in her bank work and she resigned. Tom Boright Jr., of the Commercial West, came into my office immediately afterward and I told him of the incident. He always kidded me for firing a girl for making a two million dollar mistake.

Another incident involving the same girl had happened previously. One of her duties was to list and total the overdrafts from the customers' ledger. She was very slow in her work, and one little girl who was waiting for the ledger became disgusted and said: "Wake up sleeping Jesus, and get the lead out of your pants." Life is interesting around a bank.

One day we apparently had made a mistake in returning a ten dollar check of one of our customers. I noticed the customer was pretty angry about something as he was talking to one of our officers. I stepped up to see what was wrong. He said that because of our mistake, he had to take a day off from his work and would lose a day's wages. I informed him we did not want him to lose any money because of our mistake, and wrote him a check for the amount. He took the check, but soon returned, and said he would also lose his overtime for the week. I asked him how much that would be, and wrote him a new check including overtime, and he left happy.

Deposits at the year end were $11,418,993.21.

24

Nineteen Forty Seven

I had now been a widower for more than two years and was living at the Alex Johnson Hotel. Living alone was not the most satisfactory situation. So on January 25 I married Agnes Moran Foster. I had met Agnes in the early fall. She had come to Rapid City the year before to be with her daughter and family, her son-in-law being stationed at the air base. Agnes had been a widow for the past seven years. At first we thought of each other as good company and neither one of us had any serious intentions. After we became better acquainted, I was impressed with her good background and her high character, and we decided to marry. The marriage took place at the home of the daughter, and invited to be present were her family and the parents of my son-in-law, Harris Torgerson. The pastor was Rev. Sylvan Moe.

Uninvited and present was also Herb H. Echtermeyer, vice president of the Omaha National Bank. He had come to town to make a call at our bank. I told him I was going to be married, but we had not planned on any

Our Wedding

Agnes and I

Our First Home in Rapid Canyon

We Lived Here Sixteen Years

outside guests. He said that made no difference and he was coming to the wedding, and he did. Herb and I have been good friends for many years, and close friends that we were, he became a welcome guest.

Agnes was born in Tennessee, reared in Birmingham, a true Southerner converted to a Northerner. For many years she had lived in Los Angeles. Agnes is accomplished and beautiful, and we have had a successful marriage for more than eighteen years now.

I want to tell you a little about her family. She has only one daughter, also named Agnes, but affectionately called Terry. She is married to Ray J. Binder, who spent twenty years in the U.S. Air Force and retired as a Lieutenant Colonel about two years ago. They have two children. James is now in his third year of college with dentistry as his goal. Sandra is attending high school. The family now lives at Orlando, Florida, and Agnes makes about two trips a year to visit them.

After our marriage, we lived at the Alex Johnson Hotel for several months. We decided we would modernize the cabin home I owned on Rapid Creek, six miles from the bank, and we lived there less than a year. We found we had made a mistake. It was a long drive a couple of times a day, and in the winter there was very little sunshine that reached the cabin because of its location, and it was rather a lonesome place in the winter time. In the summer it was very pleasant. We decided to build a new home at 1621 West Boulevard, where we have lived since. We are now a half interest partner in building a new seven-story, fireproof, 24-unit deluxe high-rise apartment building near downtown. We expect to move into one of the apartments about the time this book is published.

At the convention of the South Dakota Bankers Association I was elected president, an honor that came to me unexpectedly. I enjoyed my year as president, working with the many fine bankers in South Dakota.

The building boom continued. The city was spreading out, with new homes in every direction. The problem was to secure mortgage money, since there simply was not enough mortgage money in Rapid City to provide financing. We were limited by law in making mortgages to a certain percentage of our savings and time deposits. One large builder had a commitment to finance 100 houses, but when he had built 39 homes the commitment was withdrawn. He came to us and there had to be some solution. We looked for outside money and made a deal with a large insurance company to purchase the mortgages we made. That is how we got into mortgage loaning and servicing, a business that has grown big with this bank. Later we made other connections and we have sold FHA and other mortgages to other banks and to insurance companies in many states. For many years we have been the largest originator and servicer of mortgages of any bank, insurance company or other lender in South Dakota. We make the loans in the ordinary course of business for our own investment, and when we have a sufficiently large block of mortgages, we sell them. We receive one-half of one per cent of the interest collected for our service, and the mortgagor continues to do business with us and make payments monthly to us. So far we have sold more than fifty million dollars in mortgages, and our mortgage department has proved to be very profitable. We have made many friends and obtained many new accounts through our activity in this field.

We added $100,000.00 to the surplus fund giving us total capital funds of $540,394.06. We are still short of capital in relation to our deposits and this was usually a criticism on the examiner's report. At the year end our deposits were $12,982,665.83.

25

Nineteen Forty Eight

The year brought growing pains. The building which had appeared too large six years ago was no longer adequate to the space we were using. We asked the tenant we had in the rear part of the building to vacate and moved our bookkeeping department into the vacated space.

Earl Keller was promoted to Vice President, and Walter Pailing became Cashier.

Life is one constant education. You continue to learn by being alert and willing to gain knowledge from the experience of others, which may often be less costly than learning by your own experience. With this thought in mind, the bank joined the Financial Public Relations Association shortly after the bank opened for business. This is a very helpful organization, and I feel that in the early days I learned much from our membership that I used in Rapid City.

The Financial Public Relations Association have an annual national convention and it is a working convention. Everyone who attends comes to learn all he can about public relations, advertising and business promotion. After the general sessions in the morning, members gather in smaller groups to discuss various subjects of interest on the agenda. You are free to move from one group to another, and the exchange of ideas and experiences of other banks has been very valuable. The association also publishes a monthly magazine containing much of the best bank advertising from all over the nation, plus keeping the membership informed of new ideas by special mailings and bulletins.

In earlier days, I attended many of the annual conventions, but today Ronald Campbell, Vice President, who handles the Business Development department for our bank, has taken over my membership and responsibility.

Bank buildings, like people, have personalities. When you walk into a bank and find it light and cheerful, neat and clean, you receive a favorable impression from the general appearance of the building.

When I was a bank examiner I walked into many banks for the first time. When I found a bank that looked messy, old magazines stacked high on the desks, and each officer's desk like a tornado had hit it, I had a good bet that the loans and their operations of the bank were also messy and bad. I was right many times. This is not always true. The bank could look messy and still be sound, but this was the exception.

When I walk into the quarters of any business and I see the desk of the manager or an officer with papers strewn all over it, I question the efficiency of the operation. A man with a messy desk makes me think he also has a disorganized mind. He may be tops, but I always wonder if he operates with an efficiency rating much less than one hundred per cent.

Deposits at the year end were $13,580,241.83.

26

Nineteen Forty Nine

This was the year of the big blizzard. Normally, Rapid City does not have much snow. The Black Hills seem to protect it, and the storms go north of it and come down fifty to a hundred miles east of here. Agnes was in Honolulu with her daughter, greeting a new granddaughter. New Year's Day was beautiful, and so mild we had the door open listening to the football games. The next day I had dinner with Mr. and Mrs. Howard Cole at Sturgis. The wind started to blow, and about four o'clock in the afternoon I decided to go home. A couple of hours later the storm was so bad that I would not have been able to drive the thirty miles home. We lived in our cabin in the canyon, and the next morning, noticing the storm, I decided I had better take along some shirts and socks when I went to the bank. That evening it was impossible to go home and I checked into the hotel. The next morning there was really a storm. I walked between the drifts to the bank, some as high as the store fronts, and I had a pleasant day working on the figures for the past year. Not a single customer came to the bank that day, nor did any of our help. It took a week to dig out, and it was a month before the Milwaukee Railroad was able to open their line. It was an unforgettable snowstorm, and we have been fortunate in not having anything like it since.

It was a nice morning on March 12. The telephone rang. It was my daughter calling from the hospital at Fort Ord, California, all excited. She had, within the hour, given birth to Dianne and everything was fine. Now I had a granddaughter and I was delighted. Dianne is now a junior at University High School in Los Angeles. She is a beautiful girl and has grown a little taller than her mother.

Have you ever received an anonymous letter? As far as I can recollect, I have received two. It was perhaps this year that I received the first one. I came down to work on a beautiful morning in anticipation of a nice day. I sat down to my desk and the first thing I spotted was a letter in a small envelope marked "Personal." A person is always curious when he receives a letter marked personal. This letter was unsigned. It was from a lady — I presume a lady — berating me for walking in front of a woman, and she said I did not have any manners or courtesy. Now I know better, but how and when it happened, I do not know. I had no intention of offending the lady, and I apologize to her. I hope she felt better after writing the letter, but it is no way to start a morning.

Things like that do not bother me any more, and I soon forget such incidents. I do not worry any more. I did so much worrying when I was at Toronto, and I have a new philosophy about worrying. I learned this fact the first year the bank opened. I had made a loan of $300.00 to a local man whose credit was just in between. I woke up in the middle of the night and worried about the payment of the loan, because then we had no reserves and profits to charge a bad loan to. Who should come in the first thing in the morning? The man I had worried about. So I have concluded that ninety-nine out of a hundred things we worry about never happen. So why spend time wearing oneself out worrying about something that will likely not happen. Instead, I want to save my energy to handle the thing that does happen. When I have troubles or something that disturbs me at the bank, and there can be many, I usually dismiss it from my mind and I do not take it home with me. And if I have problems, I do not feel sorry for myself, but reason that I am paid to solve problems, otherwise perhaps I would not be needed.

The second anonymous letter came quite recently. We had placed an advertisement in the newspaper offering to rent some vacant office space in the building. The sender cut out the ad and wrote across the front: "ANOTHER UN-ETHICAL DEAL. Dahl, you are famous for using your clients' money in your deals whereby you become a competitor of your clients. Even a skunk uses more ethics, he uses his own resources." I did not know it was unethical to rent vacant space in our building. This time I think I know who wrote the letter. The writer has a habit of addressing the name, both on the envelope and in the salutation, in a peculiar way. It is very similar to another letter with his name on it, and the print looks as if it came from the same typewriter. I hope he received the satisfaction he wanted by writing the letter.

Writing letters in the heat of anger can be dangerous and can backfire. I have written critical letters, left them on my desk for a day or so, and have thrown them in the wastebasket. Such letters do not look so good later, nor do I feel so critical.

This reminds me of the shortest letter I ever received. We subscribe to PRATT'S LETTER, a weekly letter written in Washington about matters of interest to bankers. The writer must be a highly educated man, for he used so many big and unfamiliar words that I have to use a dictionary to decipher the letter. I wrote to the publishers asking them to use everyday words I could understand, and I received the following answer:

PRATT'S LETTER

Washington, D. C.

Mr. A. E. Dahl, President
Rapid City National Bank
Rapid City, South Dakota
    Amen.

Yours very truly
PRATT'S LETTER

I think they took the suggestion. At least I found their letters more readable.

I now recall a letter I wrote to Senator Norbeck on February 4, 1931, when I was in Castlewood. They were having hearings in Washington on banking and improvements in the banking laws. It seemed that reflections were cast upon the small banks. I argued that the small bank could be just as strong and safe as the large bank. The letter was lengthy and I supplemented much information about our bank, the Citizens State Bank of Castlewood, and the service it was performing. I was very much surprised when Senator Norbeck had my letter printed in full in the report of the hearings. Then I received the following letter from George C. Cutler, vice president of the Guaranty Trust Company of New York:

On going through the Hearings before the Subcommittee on Banking, I came across your letter to Senator Norbeck. I don't think I have ever read a more interesting letter nor one whose contents were expressed more clearly. It seems to me you have analyzed your bank with a degree of care and intelligence which is lacking in many quarters where one would expect at least as high a degree of intelligence. I am simply writing to express my pleasure, and to add that if you chance to be in New York, it would give me great pleasure if you would call upon me and have luncheon with me.

I think it was one of the nicest letters I have received. At that time I did not have the money to travel to New York, so I was never able to accept the invitation to lunch.

It was in this year that John Ryan moved to Rapid City to be president of the First National Bank of the Black Hills. I had known John for many years. I always regarded him as a very competent banker and a good competitor. He and I were always the best of friends, and he has my highest respect.

The year 1949 was another busy year for the bank. Our mortgage department was especially busy. During the year the bank handled eighty-four per cent of all the FHA loans made in Rapid City, according to the recordings at the Court House. We had a very important part in providing mortgage money for home owners.

We transferred $100,000.00 from the undivided profit account to surplus. Deposits at the year end were $14,-363,352.56.

27

Nineteen Fifty

This year Agnes and I decided to take a vacation in Honolulu and also to visit her daughter and her family. Terry's husband, Captain Ray Binder, was stationed at Hickam Field. We sailed to Honolulu on the Lurline, one of the fine ships going to the island. We had a delightful time. Terry and Ray were gracious hosts, and we saw more of the island than most tourists. One evening while we were having dinner the telephone rang. Agnes answered. It was her nephew, Commander C. N. Kicker, USN, who was serving as an aide to the Admiral of the Fleet at Honolulu. I gathered from the conversation that I had an invitation to spend the next day on a submarine. I protested that I was not interested in going out on the ocean in a submarine, but the arrangements had been made for Captain Binder and me to be guests the next day, so with some misgivings I decided to go.

At seven o'clock the next morning we boarded the submarine and out into the Pacific we went. I was taken on a tour of the submarine, and of course everything was very crowded with mechanical equipment and living quarters. I was shown a large board with perhaps a hundred or more lights both red and green. They called it their Christmas tree. It was explained to me that when all the lights turned to green the submarine was ready to submerge, which we did just below the surface with the periscope above the water. I was also told that the submarine had been in the dry dock for more than a month, so the first job they had to perform was to balance it. This took some time. Later they had target practice by shooting compressed air instead of torpedoes. By this time I was over my nervousness. Life in a submarine is very quiet with no feeling of motion.

At noon we were served a big meal and as guest of honor I was seated next to the commanding officer in a small dining room. After dinner I had a feeling of a call to duty and I asked where the accommodations were. We went down on the lower level, and aft in the submarine I was shown the location. As I was seated I looked at the wall to my left and I began to read the instructions: Close valve one and open valve two, pull lever, close valve two and close valve one, and so on. This began to look complicated, and I did not want to do the wrong thing and sink the submarine or have water shoot up and blow me off the seat. Soon I spotted a sailor coming along and asked him to operate the gadgets, which he did, solving my predicament, and I felt relieved in more ways than one.

I was next told that before returning to shore they were going to take the submarine down to test it for leaks, and I began to wonder how deep we were going. I watched the instrument panel until it stopped at a little more than three hundred feet below the surface. Fortunately there were no leaks, and we soon returned to the surface. We proceeded into the harbor, and I stood on the small top deck as we moved past the sunken battleship Arizona. It was three o'clock in the afternoon when I set foot on the ground, happier for a wonderful experience. A few days later we were invited to join the Admiral's party to the Chinese New Year festivities. Agnes, Terry and Mrs. Kicker were dressed for the occasion in colorful silk coats. A photographer who spotted them asked permission to take their picture. I lined up with the girls, but was soon told I was not wanted. The next day the picture appeared on the front page of the daily newspaper.

We had planned to return on the Lurline, but Agnes and Terry wanted us to stay a few days longer and return by air, and as usual the girls won, and I saved about $150.00, the difference in fares. Midway over the ocean we were told we would probably not be able to land in Los Angeles because of the smog. We landed at Palmdale at midnight, but had to wait for buses to come. With that delay and the time spent traveling to Los Angeles, it was four o'clock in the morning by the time we were in bed.

We had now been in business sixteen years, and during this time we had never found any dishonesty among our employees, but this year we had our first attempted embezzlement. The girl involved operated one of our proof machines, which was then located immediately behind the tellers. The proof machine sorts and lists the checks to the bookkeepers. One evening one of our bookkeepers was short $500.00 in the amount of checks charged to her. At first we did not give it much thought, thinking it was an error or lost check. Mr. Gilbret Ellwein, assistant cashier, took it upon himself to find what was wrong. He knew that the missing item was cashed at teller's window number three. The teller could not remember whom she had cashed the check for. He found from the teller's proof, tracing the checks we did have, the names of the persons who had cashed a check before and after the missing check. He called these persons,

The American National Bank of Rapid City commissioned Artist Bernard Thomas to create an eighty foot Mural Painting to symbolize the area of South Dakota. This huge painting seemed an appropriate setting for this South Dakota narrative. Detailed sections from the design are pictured here,

and upon the end-sheets. The expressive story of the painting was reviewed by one writer in these words:

"In South Dakota, banking, agriculture, and natural resources form a vital team. The bank is linked closely with manufacturing, travel, vacationing tourists, mining, lumbering and military installations, as well as the sportsman's fields of hunting and fishing.

"These rich areas of production have provided Artist Bernard Thomas with excellent material with which to portray the character of this colorful area in his expansive mural. With great skill he has woven his images into a pageant of past and present. Dinosaurs, indians, and pioneers of the hazy past contrast with today's ranchers, farmers, lumbermen and tourists, who symbolize the present makers of South Dakota's wealth. And the state's

natural beauty provided a backdrop of mountains, prairies, trout streams and forests.

"This is Banker Dahl's Dakota, where for almost half a century he has lived and served his people. It is a land for which he feels a deep attachment, a land of continuing challenge and opportunity, an area of ever greater promise for the future."

e.m.k.

asking them who stood behind or in front of them at the teller's window that day. At first they did not remember, but l a t e r in the day a lady called and s a i d the person in front of her had talked to the operator of the proof machine. Then the teller remembered she had cashed a $500.00 check for the husband of the proof machine operator. They did have an account in the bank for more than the $500.00 check, so there was no question about cashing the check. About this time we received a telegram from the California Bank, in Los Angeles, informing us that there was another $500.00 check missing among the items sent to them. When we traced this back, we found a check of this amount had also been cashed that day at teller's window number two, and the check was also one paid to the husband of our proof operator. The cat was out of the bag. Our employee, the proof machine operator, had listed both checks to balance, but she had destroyed the checks. When confronted with the evidence, she blew up and asked one of our officers: "How did you get your start in life?" She paid back all the money, but both she and her husband were sentenced in Federal Court to one year in the penitentiary, with the sentence suspended on good behavior. What a price to pay.

We have had only one other embezzlement, which happened only a couple of years ago. We hired a young girl who worked behind the tellers' windows, and one of her duties was to take the mortgage loan payments that came in on the tubes from the drive-in bank to our loan tellers. When we sent delinquent notices to our mortgage borrowers, they called us and informed us they had made the payments. All were paid at the drive-in windows. We knew something was wrong, but at first we did not know where. We found that when the mortgage payments came in on the tube in cash, the girl kept the money and destroyed the payment ticket. We called in the FBI to run down the evidence, and this young girl also received a suspended sentence from the Federal Court. The young girl came from a good family in another part of the state, and had worked with us only a short time before the embezzlement. The bonding company paid the loss of about $500.00.

Embezzlement in a national bank is a federal crime. When an embezzlement occurs, we have no choice but to report it to the FBI and the national banking department. It matters not if the embezzlement is small and is repaid. If we do not report it, we will be guilty of a crime, concealing an embezzlement. A banker friend of mine in Nebraska had a difficult time after failing to report an embezzlement. One of the men in his bank embezzled money, and when caught, repaid it. My friend neglected to report the embezzlement, and when the FBI and the national banking authorities found out about it, they came to see him about his failure to do so. He had a hard time satisfying them that there was no intent to violate the law.

I feel the management has a great responsibility in preventing embezzlements. First, we try to select officers and staff with sound backgrounds, coming from good homes. We owe them a living salary so they can live decently. We must operate our banks with proper audits and controls to detect wrong-doing early. We should not be sloppy in operating our banks so that embezzlement is a temptation. We know the living habits of our officers and older employees in the most responsible positions, and we know they are not extravagant and do live within their means. I have always said a person who cannot handle his own finances and budget cannot handle the money of our customers. I regret that it has been necessary on one or two occasions to ask for the resignation of an employee who could not make ends meet. In this bank we have a full-time auditor who continuously audits and checks the work of our staff. He will monthly, at unexpected times, count the cash in the tellers' windows, and run proofs of the books and records of the bank.

Banks today carry insurance against embezzlements, robbery, and other risks. In our bank it is more than a half million dollar bond, and in addition we have a million dollar excess embezzlement bond, making a total of one and one-half million dollar bond to protect us in the event of an embezzlement. I feel confident our staff is honest, and we may never need it, but it is a protection that is there in the event of need.

This year I was honored by being elected president of the Rapid City Rotary Club. I have been a Rotarian for more than thirty years, and I have always valued my membership in the club and the opportunity to break bread with a large number of fine fellows once a week.

Russell Halvorson, who joined the bank two years previously, was elected assistant cashier.

Each year since the bank was organized, our deposits have increased, and this year was no exception. Our year-end deposits were $15,147,513.47.

28

Nineteen Fifty One

In the middle of the year we received a very sharp letter from L. A. Jennings, First Deputy Comptroller of the Currency, demanding we increase our capital by sale of new stock. We had capital funds of $862,656.67 to $17,003,774.96 in deposits, a ratio of about five per cent. We knew we were under-capitalized. We also knew we would have no trouble selling an additional amount of stock; however, it would not make us any more money, but result in a dilution of our earnings to investment. We were equally determined that we were not going to sell any more capital stock. Our bank was in excellent condition, and there was no criticism of our loans and operation. We had good earnings and we were using the greater part of the earnings building the capital. We replied to the letter, explaining our position and asked that we be permitted to build our capital from earnings. We did not receive a reply letter, and this was the last time any request was made to increase the capital by a stock sale. To this date we have not received any further requests, and today we are in a strong capital position.

We had some more growing pains and remodeled our basement and moved our bookkeeping department downstairs.

Kiting checks is one trouble around a bank that makes the banker's hair turn gray. If they are large, they could result in a big loss for the bank. Fortunately we have not had many such incidents, but we are always on the lookout for the check kiter. Check kiting occurs when a customer — or perhaps I should say a crook — starts floating checks between banks. A kiter will open an account in three or more banks. Perhaps he has two or more business accounts and one or more personal accounts he controls. Or perhaps he may connive with another person to float checks between them. The opportunity to make check kiting possible is best when the banks are in two or more cities. A bank in Iowa a few years ago sustained a loss of many thousands of dollars on a check kite.

There was a young man in Rapid City who had a couple of small business accounts, and he opened an account in all three banks in Rapid City. He started to float the checks between the banks in a big way within a short time. When the bubble burst, he owed the three banks more than six thousand dollars, and it looked as if we were in for a big loss. Fortunately for us, but very sad for the family, his mother drove all night from Iowa, and at a meeting with representatives from all three banks, she threw on the table some United States Savings Bonds and said: "Here is my life's savings." There were tears around the table, but it did not undo the damage the son had done to his loving mother who saved him from the penitentiary.

I remember a married woman who had lived in Rapid City and had an account with us. She moved with her husband to Oregon and opened an account with a bank there. She also had an account in her home town in Kentucky. She commenced floating checks between the three

149

banks and when we discovered what was going on, she had us stuck for nine hundred dollars. We talked to the banker in her home town and he was surprised, saying she came from a good family. We called her on the telephone and demanded our money. She wanted a few days' time, and we received our money, no doubt from her family.

Mr. Shoberg, senior vice president, caught a check kite a few years ago when, in opening the mail, he noticed a small wholesale firm in Iowa was regularly sending $5,000 to $10,000 to their account with us. Now why should they be sending money here? It seemed more likely the money should be sent to Iowa from their sales here. He investigated and found a kite going. Fortunately for us, we had been paid on all checks deposited with us, so we returned the checks drawn on us. We figured out the actual balance, wrote a cashier's check for the amount, sent it to the company, and told them the account was closed.

When a check kite occurs, the first bank to discover it usually comes out the best. The bank has an opportunity to collect the deposited checks and returns the checks drawn on the account.

At this time I am reminded of an incident that happened many years ago to Earl Keller, now senior vice president. We had a no-good note we had not been able to collect. I sent Earl to see the borrower. He was greeted by the family dog, and by the time he came back to his car, he had lost a good part of his pants. I called the debtor, and told him what had happened, and said we wanted our money. I guess I scared him, for he came to the bank and paid the note in full. I think we have a few more notes we will be glad to exchange for a pair of pants.

Our deposits on Dec. 31, 1951, were $17,003,774.96.

29

Nineteen Fifty Two

I have always had the highest respect for the national bank examiners. They are capable men, and it is always a pleasure to have them come. This year I had my first blow-up with an examiner. It was on April 21, that John Sweeney, national bank examiner, came to the bank. He had examined the bank five times previously, and once since. I always considered him a capable examiner, and still do, but this morning he must have had the wrong breakfast or something. Our first difference came over a loan of $80,000.00 on some wool stored in a warehouse. Although the price of wool had dropped since we made the loan, we still had ample collateral and the borrower was a responsible man. John was going to set this loan up as sub-standard and I objected. I explained the borrower was going to refinance the loan with the Commodity Credit Corporation, and it would be paid within a short time. It could not be substandard. We did not agree and the matter was not argued any further, but John stood his ground. Now if there had been only one loan we could not agree on, it would not have been too important. Then came another loan. This was a $20,000.00 loan I had made to two young men in Rapid City a few days before the examination. They were two very capable men and the business was young, but they had shown excellent earnings, although I will admit the statement did not look too good. John was going to set this loan up as substandard also. I tried to explain to him I had just made the loan and knew the circumstances and had the advantage of knowing these men, and that I felt confident they would pay as agreed. I said if the loan was not paid at the time of the next examination, he would have the right to criticize it as substandard, but not this time. He insisted it was substandard, and then I blew my top. I told him to go ahead and criticize anything he wanted to in the bank and not even show it to me, but I was going to continue to run this bank as I pleased so long as I did it legally. I apologized afterwards, but down in my heart I felt I was right, and subsequent events proved it.

The wool loan was paid in full within three months, just as I had stated. The $20,000.00 loan was also paid, and today these men can come to the bank and borrow five times this amount if they wish. Neither of these loans was substandard. This was the only time I had any differences with a bank examiner. When the examiner wants to criticize a small loan I don't object even though I may not agree with him, saving my powder for the big loan, where we may have different opinions. If the examiner wants to criticize a big loan, and I know he is right, I have no objection to the criticism.

We doubled our capital by a stock dividend, giving our shareholders one additional share for every share owned.

We were doing a big business originating FHA loans and selling them to investors; the mortgage department was very profitable. The trouble was that then Korean

152

War excess profit income taxes were taking eighty per cent of the earnings. I was thinking about organizing a separate mortgage loan corporation to handle our mortgage department and save on income taxes. I found this required a capitalization of $100,000.00.

For some years a few of our customers and some attorneys had asked our bank to have trust powers and operate a trust department. We knew many trust departments were unprofitable, and also the responsibility was great. It was then the thought came to us to kill two birds with one stone — organize a trust company to provide trust services and also handle the mortgage business. In this way the mortgage department could carry the loss developing the trust business, and also place our earnings into a lower bracket of taxation.

One morning I brought the idea of organizing a trust company to Roy Dean, chairman, and Harry Devereaux, vice president. They listened, but did not display much enthusiasm to my idea. My suggestion was to capitalize the trust company for $100,000.00 with a paid-in surplus of $20,000.00. We would offer the stock to the stockholders of the Rapid City National Bank pro-rata. The pro-rata share of Roy Dean, Harry Devereaux, and me was approximately $24,000.00 each. Roy said that if he could have a five per cent return on the investment he would be interested. Such a return would amount to $1,200 yearly or the equivalent of $100.00 a month salary. He apparently did not feel the trust company would be profitable and pay dividends.

On July 9 I called Verne Abeel, Superintendent of Banks, asking him to send us the necessary papers to organize a bank, but I did not tell him what I had in mind. I think I should explain that we do not have any statute providing for the organizing of trust companies separately from banks. The only way it could be organized was to organize a bank with trust powers.

We found the banking commission had scheduled a

meeting in Rapid City on July 24, so I planned to make the application in person. I was told the commissioners were going to be very busy, but they would give me ten minutes to present what I had in mind. The meeting was held at the Alex Johnson Hotel in the Mural Room on the second floor, and after cooling my heels in the hallway for a while, I was invited in.

Present were Verne Abeel, Superintendent of Banks, O. D. Hanson, Paul Jones, and the late J. F. Holdhusen, members of the State Banking Commission. Also present was Charles Alden, Chief Supervisor, FDIC, for this district.

I presented two documents to the commission. One was entitled "Notice of Intention to organize and file Articles of Incorporation for a State Bank." The second document was "Articles of Incorporation of the Rapid City Trust Company." These papers were identical with papers used to incorporate a state bank. The preamble reads: "Know All Men By These Presents: That we, the undersigned, do hereby associate ourselves together for the purpose of forming a banking corporation, etc." The Articles refer to "Bank" no less than four times.

The reason I quote in detail above is that I was to find out later that the banking commission did not know we were applying for a bank charter with trust powers. I am sure Verne Abeel knew, because all the papers were before him, and his long experience with the banking department must have given him the knowledge that this was a bank application.

I was greeted cordially, but they did not bother to look at the two documents, and after a few minutes they approved the application. I did tell them we did not intend to conduct a commercial banking business, but to confine our deposits to trust deposits, escrow deposits, and time certificates of deposit. I further stated we planned to make only real estate and FHA loans in the trust company. I am sure they would have known it was a bank charter we were applying for if they had taken a look at the two documents, but they did not bother to do so. There was no misrepresentation of any kind, and the fact that they acted quickly, without so much as to look at the papers, was no fault of mine, but they apparently were in a hurry to adjourn the meeting.

Naturally, I was a little surprised myself at the quick approval. I thought they were a grand group of people, and I gave it no further thought. I surely thought that as members of the commission they were familiar with the banking laws of South Dakota.

On August 1, 1952, the Secretary of State issued the charter for the Rapid City Trust Company. We also decided to apply for membership in the Federal Deposit Insurance Corporation and the Federal Reserve System so there would be no confusion because of the fact we were to occupy the same building. In due time these applications were approved, and nearly two months after the banking commission had approved the charter, the Rapid City Trust Company opened for business on September 15, 1952. A news release published in the local papers read:

RAPID CITY TRUST COMPANY
OPEN FOR BUSINESS

The Rapid City Trust Company opened for business September 15. It was organized and capitalized by the stockholders of the Rapid City National Bank and has the same Board of Directors and officers.

It was chartered and organized under the state laws of South Dakota and is a state bank with trust powers. It has a capital of $100,000.00 and a surplus of $20,000.00.

It will temporarily occupy space in the Rapid City National Bank Building. Spacious new quarters will be provided in the rear of the bank building with entrance on Seventh Street.

It is the only trust company or bank with trust powers in western South Dakota. The Rapid City Trust Company will act as trustee, administer estates, act as guardians, and such other duties generally performed by trust departments. It will also originate and service FHA and First Mortgage loans sold to investors. It will not handle checking or savings accounts, nor will it make commercial loans. It will issue time certificates of deposits. It is a member of the Federal Reserve System and the Federal Deposit Insurance Corporation.

A. E. Dahl, president, said: There is an opportunity and definite need for a trust company here. With the growing wealth and increased population of this area, we are confident the trust company will have an important part in this community and render a useful service that will gain in importance in years to come.

I was elected Trust Officer of the company and, with my legal background, I felt confident I could handle the office on a temporary basis until we could find an experienced trust man to take this important position.

Everything was going along nicely until I attended the American Bankers Convention in New York in October. I was told that on a special train carrying Minnesota and South Dakota bankers to the convention, a South Dakota banker criticized O. D. Hanson for granting another bank charter in Rapid City. That the Rapid City Trust Company was a bank was apparently news to Mr. Hanson. My informant told me I was possibly in trouble with the banking commission.

On November 15 I was called to Pierre before the banking commission. They presented me with an Amendment to the Articles of Association that limited our powers to trust business with a limitation on the time certificates we could take, and also excluded us from doing any commercial banking business.

I had no objection to the amendment as that was our intention all along, but I said I would have to take it to our attorneys for their approval.

The banking commission frankly admitted they did not know what they were doing in granting the charter. They thought it was only a trust charter, and not a bank; because the title did not include the word "Bank," they did not know it was a bank. The banking laws of South Dakota do not provide that a bank must have the word bank in the title. There are many prominent banks all over the United States that do not have the word bank in their name.

Our attorneys objected to the amendment. They said we would amend the trust company out of business. The laws of the state say what we are and what powers we have, and an amendment would cast a cloud on our charter. We were on the spot. We were in agreement with the banking commission as to limiting the business we proposed to do in the trust company, but legally we could not comply with their request. We advised the banking commission we could not pass the amendment and furnished them with the legal opinions. We maintained a friendly attitude to the commission and wanted to cooperate with them, but they should not ask us to do the impossible. We heard nothing further for many months and we thought our troubles were over. We were mistaken, as will be seen in the next chapter.

The Rushmore State Bank moved to Rapid City from Hill City on October 17 this year and opened as the third bank in Rapid City. We had no objection since we knew that sooner or later there would be a third bank in Rapid City, and we welcomed them to Rapid City.

Our year-end deposits were $17,917,170.93, and the trust company had deposits of $207,655.89.

30

Nineteen Fifty Three

Early in the year 1953 we completed the remodeling of the last fifty feet of our building into beautiful quarters for the trust company. We provided a beautiful room to be used for a conference room which also doubled as a directors' room.

We secured the services of Eugene Pester to be trust officer. He came to us from the First Trust Company, Lincoln, Nebraska, where he had several years of trust experience. Eugene is deceased now, but he was a brilliant man and did much valuable work for us in building the trust business on a sound, profitable basis.

When the building was built, we had not anticipated the growth we would have, and this year we also had to make some more changes. Originally our vault in the center of the building was in two parts, one for the safe deposit boxes and the other for the bank vault, separated by an eighteen-inch wall of solid concrete. Pressed for more room for safe deposit boxes, we decided to build another vault for the bank's use in the rear of the building, and take out the separating wall. The safe deposit vault would be twice as large. Roy Dean said it could not be done. With considerable work and mess, we did, and nobody was more pleased than Roy.

This year we purchased three lots diagonally back from the bank to provide parking for our customers. We tore down an old historic home on the property, black-topped the lot, and the result was a very fine parking lot. Our customers were pleased.

In May I attended the South Dakota Bankers Convention in Huron. Up ot this time we had heard nothing further from the banking commission, but their silence came to an end. I was summoned to come to a room in the Marvin Hughitt Hotel, where the commission was in session, and they demanded action on the proposed amendment in no uncertain terms.

In the meantime, Roy Fenner had been appointed Superintendent of Banks. Roy had been with the banking department for many years as an examiner, but for a short time he was an officer in the Sioux Valley Bank in Sioux Falls. He was now back heading the department, and I presume he thought he could do something about forcing the amendment, where the commission had failed. Roy Fenner and O. D. Hanson did all the talking. I felt the other two commissioners did not care much, but they went along.

Now O. D. Hanson is a very fine man and a good banker. I like him. I think he can be very reasonable, and in other banking matters I have found him cooperative. I felt that in the matter before the commission, if it had been he and I, we could have come to an agreement. But there must have been tremendous pressure on O. D. from some source, that he would pursue a lost cause and demand the impossible. Probably he was trying to save face.

The proposed amendment was watered down and less severe, but I felt quite sure our attorneys would not approve it. What should we do? We probably could have told the commission to jump in the lake, and our attorneys assured us there was nothing the commission could do about it. On the other hand, we wanted to cooperate with the commission if it was possible. I told them I would submit the amendment to our attorneys and place the question before the stockholders, but doubted its passage.

We called a special stockholders' meeting for July 16 and submitted the amendment for their approval. One attorney wrote us: "If you pass the amendment it will be necessary we withdraw such designation of your trust company as has been made and to refrain from making any further designations in the future." There was only one answer, the stockholders refused to pass the amendment.

I wrote the banking commission of the result in the nicest way I could put words together, saying it was impossible to pass the amendment and was hopeful the commission would not press the matter any further.

We did not have to wait very long. On August 12, about four o'clock in the afternoon, the telephone rang, and I was informed that I was wanted for an appearance before the commission in session at Gill's Motel in Rapid City. Harry Devereaux happened to be in the bank and went along. After greetings of the day, Superintendent of Banks Roy Fenner read us the following resolution the commission had passed:

WHEREAS, an application was made by A. E. Dahl, and others, the officers and principal stockholders of the Rapid City National Bank at Rapid City, South Dakota, for a corporate charter from the State of South Dakota, to engage in the business of a trust company under the firm name of "Rapid City Trust Company," Rapid City, South Dakota, and

WHEREAS, this Commission and the said incorporators or organizers of the Rapid City Trust Company have failed to agree upon the terms of the Articles of Incorporation, particularly Article Two, limiting the purposes and powers of the corporation to the operation of a trust company, exercising only trust powers, with the exception of the authority to issue and negotiate time certificates of deposit in an amount not exceeding five hundred thousand dollars, at one time, and

WHEREAS, the said incorporators or organizers have filed in the office of the Secretary of State, purported Articles of Incorporation without the same having first been approved by this Commission, as required by SDC 6.0304 and is illegally operating and conducting a trust business within the meaning of SDC 6. 05,

BE IT THEREFORE RESOLVED that this matter be referred to the Attorney General of this state for investigation, and that he be authorized and directed to take legal proceedings on behalf of the state to enjoin and restrain the said Rapid City Trust Company from continuing to operate as a bank and trust company until such time as Articles of Incorporation are presented in such form as the Commission deems proper and which this Commission may approve.

Upon roll call the vote was as follows:

Mr. O. D. Hanson   "aye"
Mr. J. F. Holdhusen   "aye"
Mr. F. A. Olson   "aye"

Motion carried unanimously and declared adopted.

Just as quickly as Mr. Fenner had concluded reading the above resolution and almost in the same breath, he made the following amazing statement: "I understand

DEPARTMENT OF BANKING AND FINANCE

STATE OF SOUTH DAKOTA
PIERRE

ROY H. FENNER
SUPERINTENDENT OF BANKS

August 26, 1953

Mr. A. E. Dahl, President
Rapid City Trust Company
Rapid City, South Dakota

Dear Mr. Dahl:

In reference to the matter of approval of amendments to your charter as
discussed at various times with the State Banking Commission and in
particular at Rapid City on August 12th, I wish to inform you that the
Commission has now instructed me to give you their alternatives to the
solution of the situation, which are as follows:

1. That the Attorney General start proceedings against
    the Rapid City Trust Company according to the resolution
    passed by the State Banking Commission on August 12,
    1953.

2. That the Rapid City Trust Company comply with the
    request of the Commission to amend their articles as
    proposed.

3. That the Commission allow ample time for the Rapid
    City National Bank to apply for trust powers and
    absorb the business of the Rapid City Trust Company
    and dissolve their corporate existence, provided that
    such intent is made known to the Commission.

4. That the matter is in the hands of the Attorney
    General and any settlement will have to be made with
    him.

If you propose to follow the provisions of proposal 2 or 3, or will
immediately negotiate with the Attorney General for a settlement as
provided by proposal 4, you should notify this office of such intent.
Otherwise the Attorney General will be notified to proceed immediately.

Yours very truly

Superintendent of Banks

that when this resolution is given the Attorney General it will be given to the press." Now what was the commission trying to do? They must have agreed in advance that Fenner should make this statement. Were they trying to scare "hell" out of us? Did they lack confidence that they could do anything about it, and so resorted to scare tactics and threats?

At this time I had lost all my patience, and asked if that was all. They answered "yes," and I remarked, "Let the chips fall where they may," and walked out.

It was no use trying to be reasonable with the commission. The next day Harry Devereaux and I drove to Pierre, and laid the resolution and other supporting documents on the desk of Governor Sigurd Anderson. We told him we had been in business in Rapid City for twenty years, and this was the first time anyone had accused us of illegality and we resented it.

Governor Anderson was a lawyer, and understood the problem. I am quite sure he realized his banking commission was on the wrong track. He said he would see what he could do to settle the matter. When I returned home, we found the adjoining letter from the Superintendent of Banks on my desk.

I immediately wrote the Governor the following letter:

> Here is a photostatic copy of a letter we received today. This letter no doubt was written before you have had an opportunity to look into the matter.
>
> We are surprised and amazed. This letter, together with the threat made by the Superintendent of Banks at the August 12th meeting to give the matter to the press, makes it appear that unless we pass the requested amendment, there is a determination to ruin the Rapid City Trust Company.

163

We cannot pass the amendment and stay in business if we lose the confidence of the legal profession upon whom we are almost wholly dependent for trust business.

The resolution implying "illegality" also disturbs us very much. The allegation we have filed articles not approved by the state banking commission is refuted by their written approval on the articles of association. We have built the largest banking business in Rapid City upon honorable methods, and this is the first time we have been accused of any illegality.

We hope this matter will have your careful consideration and an early determination.

A couple of weeks later we received a letter from the Governor stating the banking commission had withdrawn their request for an amendment to the articles, and they would be satisfied if we amended the by-laws stating we would not transact a commercial banking business.

We submitted the proposed by-law to the attorneys. They said such a by-law was likely unconstitutional, but it would be of no effect. In order to help the Governor with his banking commission, we agreed to pass the by-law.

There was one condition, however, we demanded. We said we would not pass the by-law until the banking commission passed a reolution erasing from the record the resolution passed accusing us of illegality. They agreed, but passed first a resolution with several "whereases" that we had complied with their request, etc. We sent word back to the Governor that such a resolution was not satisfactory, but we wanted the commission to pass a resolution simply erasing it from the record, and not one that left the impression we had been wrong and agreed to their requests. The banking commission finally agreed to pass the simple resolution we requested. We then passed the by-law.

After Governor Anderson had left office, about a year later, C. G. Skartvedt, one of our stockholders who had voted "no" at the stockholders' meeting, brought an action against the Rapid City Trust Company to test the legality of the amendment to the by-laws. The action was brought in the Pennington County Circuit Court, and the Judge ruled the amendment unconstitutional.

Now we were back just where we had started. The Rapid City Trust Company was a full-fledged bank and could transact any banking business it desired. We never did take advantage of the additional powers. We kept our word to the commission that we would not transact any commercial business, but we confined the business in the trust company to the trust business and mortgage department. The banking commission did not win anything, but all they did was to cause us trouble and expense. So endeth the controversy.

On October 17 Roy Dean died suddenly and I lost a good friend who was largely responsible for my being here. It was Roy Dean who spearheaded the organization of the Rapid City National Bank. Roy was probably one of the most popular men in the bank with the staff and employees. He was not very busy and had time to visit with them. There were many tears among the employees who attended his funeral. He had a regular routine. He would usually appear at the bank at nine in the morning. He would sit in his office reading his mail and magazines. Then he would make his rounds in the bank, and at noon he would go to the Elks Club and play cards. He would return to the bank about three o'clock in the afternoon, pick up his mail and go home. After returning home, he would usually take his wife Burgess for a ride around town. In the evening he would listen to his favorite radio program, and watch

TV in later years, and if it was his favorite, you could not get him out for the evening.

Roy Dean started in life working for a contractor in Sioux City. One day he told his boss he was going to get married and file on a claim on some land near Marcus, South Dakota. The boss, taller than Roy, looked down on him and said: "I guess you have as much right to starve a woman as anyone else." Little did he know the success Roy would be. Later he operated a grocery store at Marcus, made some money, and came to Rapid City. For several years he had the Chevrolet agency here, and then retired, until he got into the local liquidation fight and later the organization of the bank. After that Roy never did want to venture into further investments, and his account at the bank year in and year out was over $100,000.00.

Some people did not understand Roy. He would sometimes, perhaps in fun, make some crazy statement without foundation. He was easily swayed in his thinking, and the last man who talked with him had him converted to his thinking. There was one thing nobody could sway him on, and that was to talk him into an unsound deal that would cost him money. He took great interest in the affairs of the bank. He usually formed an opinion on everything quickly, and although we did not always agree, I found him reasonable and willing to concede if he was wrong. Roy was an unusual man, and I valued his friendship.

In the first full year of operation, the trust company had good earnings, paid a dividend to the stockholders, and at the year end had accumulated $32,194.51 in undivided profits. It was a success in every way beyond our hopes. We also developed a nice trust business. At the year end our deposits were $18,050,901.46 in the bank and $666,720.40 in the trust company.

31

Nineteen Fifty Four

The parking lot was a great success, but what we needed was a drive-in bank on the lot. Under South Dakota law, building a drive-in bank on the lot separate from the building might be construed as a branch. We came up with the thought that if we connected the drive-in bank with a tunnel so it became a part of our building, this technicality would not apply. The Comptroller of Currency had no objection, but he suggested we obtain an opinion from the Attorney General. We did, and the opinion was favorable to our plan. He said that with a connecting tunnel, the drive-in would become an extension of our building, and there would not be any violation of the branch bank laws of South Dakota.

This was good news. We erected a small building with one drive-up window and one open walk-up window. We opened up the street and built the tunnel. We had a little difficulty avoiding sewer, telephone and water lines. The tunnel may be a little crooked and up and down, but it served the purpose. It also became useful for our tellers in going and coming from the drive-in bank. We also installed a pneumatic tube to carry checks and currency to and from the drive-in.

We celebrated the opening of the drive-in by having "Tunnel Day." We invited everyone and gave one dollar to every hundredth visitor and ten dollars to every thousandth visitor. It was a great success and people streamed through the tunnel all day.

One of the things that have brought us business over the years is that we give more authority to our tellers to cash checks that come over the counter than do many banks. I know our tellers are intelligent and have as many brain cells in their heads as do the officers. So we authorize the tellers to cash checks from people in this community if the amount is reasonable and it is their judgment that the check is good. Contrast this with some banks where the tellers have little or no authority. The teller informs the person at the window that inasmuch as he does not have an account, he will have to have an officer's okay. He waits for the officer, then waits again at the teller's window, and leaves the bank with a bad feeling. The hardest job we have is to bring people to our front door. When they come we should serve them well and invite them to return. After a while they think we are a pretty good bank and open their account with us. We play the law of averages. Sure, we make a mistake and receive a bad check now and then, but the loss has been nominal, and we have saved a lot of time for the officers. If the teller is in doubt or the amount is large, the check is referred to the officers.

Many years ago while visiting with my brother in Minneapolis, he said he did not have a bank account. I asked him why, and he said he did not like the way banks did business. He had gone to a bank in Minneapolis to cash his pay check and had wasted so much time obtaining an approval of his check that he now cashed his checks at the Warner Hardware Store and bought money orders to pay his bills.

One Saturday a young attractive wife was standing at the check counter endorsing her check to be cashed. Her husband was impatient, and the lines at the windows were long. He suggested they should go to the other bank where they were not so busy. She answered: "But they know me here." I overheard the conversation and enjoyed her remark.

I am sure our policy of giving more authority to our tellers has paid off many times. If people that come to our bank are treated pleasantly and served quickly, they pass the word to others, and it is the accumulative good words people say about us that bring new customers and friends.

In Rapid City we have many tourists and quite frequently we are asked to cash their checks. Now there is little profit in cashing a check for a tourist, but our experience has been that we have been able to do so without any loss. Our officers usually take this responsibility. Carl Bangert, vice president, tells me the first question he usually asks is whether they are on their way home or have just commenced their vacation. If they are going home it is understandable that they may have spent more than planned, and they are a good risk. If they have just started on their vacation, the risk is greater since they should have planned to bring along more money for their vacation.

Usually when I leave on a trip I take along enough money to bring me home again, but on occasion I have asked bankers whom I did not know to cash my check, and they have always been glad to do so. Recently I experienced an incident that irritated me. We had just returned to Los Angeles from a trip around the world, and I walked into a bank where we had carried an account for many years. My friend in the bank, whom I knew very well, was no longer with the bank. The receptionist ushered me to the same desk, now occupied by a young man who was a vice president. I gave him our bank statement with my name on it as chairman. I told him I wanted to cash a check for two hundred dollars. He did not answer, "Sure" or "Glad to do it," but said nothing. I told him we had an account with the bank and he answered: "Yes, yes, yes." I don't think he had ever heard of the American National Bank and perhaps not Rapid City. I was determined I was going to have my check cashed and wrote it out. He asked if I had any identification, and I took out my passport with my picture in it, and he agreed to cash the check. Now I don't think I look like a crook, but it was the first time in my experience that a banker has ever asked me for any identification. I took the money and quickly departed without any further conversation leading to a better acquaintance or any exchange of the pleasantries of the day. I am sure he was a very fine man, perhaps with more education than I have, but he appeared to be unsure of himself. This may be a small incident. I do not think this young man knew how to meet people, make them feel at home or how to make friends, which is all-important today.

When I was in Tokyo, Ralph Arnold, president of the First National Bank of Ontario, California, invited me to acompany him to a branch bank of the Bank of America. We were cordially greeted by an officer. After Ralph had completed his business, the officer turned to me and said: "Mr. Dahl, do you need any money?" I was not without funds, but thought it might be a good idea to have a little reserve, so I cashed a check for $200.00. We enjoyed visiting with him and about banking in Japan. Before I came back to the hotel, my wife saw some pearls she liked, so most of the $200.00 was used. Guess I was lucky I cashed the check. Or perhaps my wife was lucky I had gone to the bank.

What a difference in bankers, but I would like to say

that most bankers are capable and friendly. Along this line, when I was visiting with C. R. Gossett, president of the Security National Bank of Sioux City, many years ago, he stated that it is hard to move an account from one bank to another. So he said the first thing he did was to build a friendship with the owner of the account he would like to have. He tried to create a desire in the customer's mind that he would like to do business with Mr. Gossett's bank. Until he was able to do this, it was almost impossible to take an account away from another bank. Then, when something went wrong, as it does in every bank, possibly unintentionally, but nevertheless it failed to please the customer, he was in the golden chair to receive the business. I have always remembered this, and our bank is a soft-sell institution. We strive hard to make a favorable impression on people and create the desire Mr. Gossett mentioned to bring business to our bank. It has worked. I have many good friends in Rapid City who do not do business with this bank. And if we meet socially, I never ask them for their banking business or inquire why they do not do business with us.

The Safe Deposit Department is an important part of our business. In our Main Office we have a total of 3181 boxes, with about 90 per cent rented. We have boxes of all sizes. I have always appreciated the liability a bank has in the operation of this department, and we have surrounded it with every precaution. Our Main Office vault has eighteen inches of solid reinforced concrete on all sides, top and bottom. We have a seven-ton door, complete with time lock. The door is opened just before the bank opens for business, and is closed immediately after regular banking hours.

All our boxes have double locks, one of which can be opened by the customer, and the other by a guard key of the bank, and it always takes two keys to open the box. If the customer loses his key, the only way the box can be opened is to drill the lock. There are no

171

duplicate keys anywhere. All our keys are unnumbered. If a key is lost there is no way to tell which box it will open. Before we re-rent a box to another customer, the lock is moved to another box, so the original key that would open the box before will no longer work in that particular box.

I remember an experience I had a long time ago when we were still in our first banking quarters. A man came to my desk and said someone had stolen $700.00 in currency from his box. I said this was impossible because he had the only key that would open the box. Oh, he said, it was not done by an employee but by someone in charge (I presume he meant me), and I am going to tell the directors. I told him that would be fine, and since two of the directors were in the basement at the time, he could go down and see them. He repeated his story that someone had stolen money from his box. We asked him to get his box, which he did. After taking out his papers, there was his $700.00 rolled with a rubber band around it. He was very much embarrassed and said: "I beg your pardon," and left.

I had another experience during the war. We were short of safe deposit boxes and did not have any to rent. A lady from Wyoming moved to Rapid City and since we did not have a box for her, she decided to share a box with her sister and was given written authority by her sister to enter and use the box. One day the Wyoming sister came to my office and said someone had stolen $1,100.00 from her box. She said she had a total of $5,000.00 in currency in the box and $1,100.00 was gone. I told her if a thief had stolen the money he would not have left $3,900.00, but would have taken it all. Besides, our contract was with her sister, and she had better take the matter up with her. It turned out that the sister had borrowed, so she said, the $1,100.00 to buy some cattle near Chadron, and that was the end of that.

I do not think there is much currency in safe deposit boxes any more because people have confidence in banks today. Many years ago an income tax evader frequently took cash for his checks at the teller's window, and then made frequent trips to this safe deposit box. We knew he was keeping currency in his box. One day the Internal Revenue agent came to my office and served us with legal papers attaching his account and the safe deposit box. We had often wondered why he was placing currency in his box at frequent intervals.

Here is a short story on the humorous side. Our safe deposit box attendant also sells U.S. Savings Bonds. A man came to buy some bonds, and Mrs. Vipond, who takes care of this department, asked: "What denomination?" He replied "Methodist." Mrs. Vipond felt like laughing, but just ignored it as if she had not heard it.

At the end of the year our deposits were $19,556,-040.24 in the bank and $718,684.59 in the trust company.

32

Nineteen Fifty Five

This was a tough year for me personally, but the year ended happily. A group of local businessmen decided Rapid City needed a country club. I was not present at the first meeting, but I was informed I was elected treasurer. I knew this was a worthy project and I accepted. Some people have the mistaken Idea that I originated the idea of building a country club. This honor belongs to William Baron, Jim Keck, and others whom I do not remember now. The amount of work and worry was more than I had bargained for. The cost of the club was far above estimates, and with trouble to obtain water, the unfortunate selection of a plastic pipe sprinkling system, and other difficulties, we were short of money to pay the bills. With help from many of the members we sold ten-year bonds, and I know for myself I put pressure on some of our good customers to buy bonds. Because they were good friends of mine I was able to convince them to buy. One day Milo Brekhus came to the bank and I invited him to have coffee next door. I said: "Milo, you are going to buy $2,000.00 in debenture bonds." He said he did not have any spare money, but I said he still had to buy the bonds. He did. All in all this project caused me many sleepless nights.

On top of this, I still had the management of the bank, listening to loan problems and making decisions. After thirty-eight years in the banking business I could not take it as I used to. My feet burned. I went to Dr. Morgan, foot specialist who prescribed arch supports, but they did not help. I went to see Dr. Jernstrom, and he could find nothing wrong with me. I sat in my office conferring with a customer, but I did not listen well, because my mind was on my burning feet, and I was wondering if the burning feet indicated there was something wrong elsewhere in my body. Finally, Dr. Jernstrom, since he could find nothing wrong, suggested I go to Rochester to see if the doctors there could find the cause.

I got the appointment, but before going to Rochester, my wife and I went East on some business, returning through Chicago. The evening before my appointment in Rochester, we had dinner at the Blackhawk Restaurant in Chicago. My feet burned so much that I had to take my shoes off. The next day in Rochester I was given a thorough physical. The doctor thought I might have circulatory troubles, but concluded I was all right. I was asked to come back again the next morning, and another doctor examined me but could find nothing wrong. Finally they told me that perhaps nerves had something to do with it, and that if I would forget that my feet burned, they probably would not burn so much. That did it. I have not had burning feet since, except at times; then I do not give it any thought, and do not register in my mind that my feet burn.

Upon returning home I did some thinking. I was nearing sixty years of age and I could not take the strain and hard work I used to be able to handle, and perhaps it would be wise to think about successor management.

At first we gave some thought to bringing in a new outside man, but we abandoned this idea. I visited Mr. Shoberg, and he did not want the presidency. Earl Keller felt the same. We had Walter Pailing, and it was unanimously agreed he should be president and take over the heavy work and I would be chairman of the board. Earl Keller was elected president of the trust company and placed in charge of the mortgage department, with Eugene Pester vice president in charge of the trust department. W. E. Shoberg was elected senior vice president. Fred Barth and Russell Halvorson were promoted to vice presidents.

It was a happy solution we had all worked together on for about a month, and every officer and director knew and had a part in arranging the new official setup. It was no longer a one-man bank, if it had ever been. The top officers had all worked together since the bank opened or shortly thereafter, and we largely thought and acted as one. We had successor management established, which is so important in banks.

It was decided that all the officers of the bank would have a meeting three mornings each week at 8:15 to review matters of importance. Walter Pailing was to have charge of the meeting. I told them I did not want to attend the meetings, because they would be inclined to look to me for answers, and I wanted the officers to make their own decisions and carry the responsibility. These meetings have continued since, usually lasting about half an hour. The senior officers remain longer and pass on new lines of credit. I drop in on the meetings now and then, particularly to report on some information I have learned of interest to the officers.

The officers carry the responsibility of making all the loans and running the bank. This experience has made them into really good bankers, and they have all done very well. I can go whenever I wish, and when I come back, I know that they have made all the necessary decisions, and that everything is in order with no worry on my part. Recently they asked if I would like to sit in on a new loan application of fifty thousand dollars. I said no. I told them that I did not want to do any collecting any more, that they would have to decide if they wanted the loan and that they would have to collect it. If they make a mistake I do not criticize them. I knew they might feel bad about a wrong decision, so why should I make them feel worse. Fortunately, they have made very few mistakes, which shows their capability to manage the bank. I feel that the way to build men is to give them lots of responsibility. Some day when I am not here, I know they will continue to do a great job. If they are not capable now, I had better find out while I am around.

This year we installed our first Time-Temperature sign. It is a service our customers and friends appreciate. I feel that it has been a good investment and has had a part in the growth of the bank. We now have five Time-Temperature signs — one at each of our bank offices. Each year we have had a contest to see who can guess nearest to the time and the day when the temperature first reaches 100 degrees. This has created a tremendous interest with thousands of entries each year. We have given a prize of $250 to the winning contestant and doubled it if the winner has an account at the bank. One year the temperature never did reach 100 degrees, so we continued the contest as a Freezer Contest, guessing the first day and the time when the sign would show a zero degree.

Up to this time our personal and installment loans had been handled by all of our officers, but the department had grown so large that we decided we should have one man in charge of it. Lyle Welsh, who had been with the Commercial Credit Corporation, was appointed to take charge of this department. He brought us much experience in handling small loans and has done a very creditable job. This department now has about five

177

thousands loans handled by Lyle and two capable assistants.

Handling personal and installment loans requires a special kind of skill. Many old-time bankers could not make these loans, because it is hard for them to realize that many people with moderate and low incomes are capable of providing for a living and making payments on a loan at the same time. I had an experience in the early days when I was making personal loans. I was going to refuse a loan because I did not think the applicant could make the payments. He flared up and told me he did not live on the boulevard because he could not afford to do so, but he lived in a modest house, his expenses were low, and his credit was just as good as mine and that of the people who lived in the large homes in other parts of the city. All anybody can do is pay on time no matter what his income. He received the loan and made all payments promptly.

A personal loan officer has to listen to all kinds of problems and is perhaps closer to and has a better understanding of the problems people have. He wants to make all the loans he can, and will often spend extra time figuring out a way to be helpful. He loans largely on character and a budgeted income. Many people with low incomes are better credit risks than others with large incomes who have a spending appetite beyond whatever they make.

It is often a great satisfaction to help people in their financial problems and see them accumulate better things for their homes and better living. Young people often start in the personal loan department and grow to where they have large credits in our commercial loan department. I have in mind one man who first started in our personal loan department but today is one of the wealthy men in Rapid City with a credit in the thousands of dollars in our commercial department.

Recently we received the following letter from a customer in our personal department. It is humorous because of the way it is written, but illustrates the problems people have. We are sympathetic in cases like this, where the customers have good intentions and want to preserve their credit but have problems beyond their control. To people who sincerely write us as this person did, we were glad to extend the payments. Here is the letter:

I received your last letter wondering why we were late. I'm sorry I should of notified you, but was in such a tangle here, didn't know which way to move. I got terrible ill, seen two different doctors and had to go through the clinic. Too ill to hold my head. Gall stones waiting out before an operation. A few days later my husband had an accident with a power saw while working 100 miles away from home & cut 3 fingers & part of the fourth on his left hand. He has been hospitalized and just started back to work. He is a foreman so he can get by with one hand. Will need surgery later on again & while my husband was in the hospital my parents were in a serious car accident, and 86 years old, a broken arm & internal injuries. I was called home which took money. This all seems crazy but its the truth. Our next payment will be late as my husband just started back to work & hasn't received any kind of compensation as yet, but we will get in as quick as he gets a check. I don't want anything to happen to our credit or our home. I am very sorry didn't notify you sooner. Be patient we will have our payment in. Thank you . . .

It must have been about this year that we got mixed up with a professional confidence man. This man opened an account with us. He said he was from Texas and had oil interests in Wyoming. He made several deposits and withdrawals, and made it a point to become acquainted with our tellers and others in the bank. He made acquaintance with businessmen around town, including the sheriff and police officers. Then about thirty days later he came in for the kill. He deposited a check of about $7,000.00 drawn on a bank in Canadian, Texas, supposedly in payment of cattle he had sold, and so marked on the corner of the check. He then went out and bought himself a Lincoln, some jewelry, and perhaps other merchandise. He came to the bank and presented a check for $3,000.00 cash. After receiving the cash, he stopped at the desk of Miss Vincent, and pointed out the window and asked her to see the new car he had purchased. He then disappeared from town. The check on Texas was a phony and we were out $3,000.00. We did not pay the other checks he gave for the car and other purchases.

I was visiting with John Haas, from Chicago, who had just arrived in Rapid City, when I was told of the incident, and then I forgot it for the day. I knew such things could happen, and we had plenty of reserves to take such losses. When I came home in the evening, I heard about it over the radio and read about it in the newspaper. If this was going to be the subject of conversation the next morning, I decided to have a meeting with the tellers. I told them that this was an honest error; that it could have happened to any one of them. If the customers kidded them about it, they were to say casually, "The boss does not seem to be worried," and laugh about it. I further told them I did not want anyone to tell which teller had cashed the check, since it was not her fault, but perhaps as much ours for not having a better system to avoid paying checks drawn against uncollected funds. The crook was caught in California with the automobile. The insurance company paid us so we did not sustain any loss.

We probably do not have the best system to prevent the payment of checks against uncollected funds. We could set up safeguards that would involve additional operating expenses, but we have played the law of averages, that any such losses would be less than the cost of the system. I know it looks silly afterwards that we would do such a stupid thing and have all the publicity, but I am satisfied that the safeguards we do have have saved us money over the long period.

Within a period of one month some years ago we had four of our tellers short $100.00 each. Where the money went we do not know, but to have four tellers short the same amount within a month leads us to believe that a short-change artist was in town. It is still a mystery how he operated. Since each teller has control over her own cash, I am sure it was some outsider that took us.

Some years ago we had an interesting experience. When checks are for $25.00 or thereabouts, our tellers cannot take the time to verify each check, so again we play the law of averages. We found we were paying a few checks of $25.00 supposedly drawn by a customer for cash, with different names but no account. We found the First National Bank was having a similar experience. There was one peculiarity about all the checks as to the way they were written. They would be drawn for twenty-five and xx/100 dollars. The two x's were prominent on all checks. So we alerted our tellers to look out for checks with two x's, but for a long time we did not receive any. Then one day a lady — perhaps crook would be a better word — presented such a check. The teller told her she would have to look up the account, and she left immediately. We called the First National Bank to alert them, and sure enough she appeared there with a similar check. The teller notified one of the officers, and she ran out the door with an officer and a customer in pursuit, through the Woolworth store, and into Landstrom's Jewelry Store, then located on Seventh Street, where she hid in the rest room. The police were called and she soon emerged. She was arrested and given a suspended sentence. She and her husband had a joint account with our bank, but she apparently wanted some spending money unbeknown to her husband.

We closed the year with further growth and our deposits were \$21,015,369.82 in the bank and \$706,642.33 in the trust company.

33

Nineteen Fifty Six

The Baken Park Shopping Center was in the planning stage and we discussed among ourselves the possibility of opening a bank in the center. We talked some of moving the charter of the Rapid City Trust Company out there. Although we had won in our fight with the banking commission, we had agreed we would not do any commercial banking business in the trust company, and we decided we would keep our agreement, although we were not legally bound any more. Furthermore, the trust company was a big success in its present location.

One day one of the state bank examiners was examining the trust company, and he dropped the remark that the Baken Park Shopping Center would be a good location for a bank. I told him if anybody was to have a bank there we would. He said we could not obtain a charter. I knew good and well the South Dakota Banking Commission would not grant us anything. I said I would not even stop in Pierre, but I would go to Washington and obtain a National charter. His remark aroused me and set me thinking that we had better get busy, because others might have the same idea about a bank in the area. I immediately boarded a plane to Minneapolis and walked into the office of Cy Upham, Chief National Bank Examiner for this district. I told him we wanted a charter for a suburban bank in Rapid City. He replied: "Good. I am glad to see an independent bank apply, since so far all the applications have come from the group banks." I asked what about going to Washington because I was in a hurry to apply. He gave me an application blank to fill out and file as soon as possible, but I did not need to go to Washington.

I returned home, filled out the application blank, and our five directors subscribed for the stock. It was our intention to permit the minority stockholders of the Rapid City National Bank to subscribe for their proportionate stock when the charter was granted. This we did, and practically all subscribed for their allotted shares.

Within about a month or so the application was granted, and we opened for business on July 2 in an old restaurant building on the Baken Park property. This was a temporary location. We built some wooden tellers' windows, and left the restaurant counter and served free coffee to the customers. One little humorous incident happened to Russell Halvorson, who was managing officer. He was at the teller's window and after taking the deposit from the receptionist for one of the doctors in the vicinity, he courteously asked her if she wanted a cup of coffee. "No, thank you," she answered icily and left. She told her employer they had a fresh young man at the bank who asked to take her out for coffee. Of course, Russell meant for her to have coffee at the coffee bar in the bank by herself.

The capital of the bank was $100,000.00, surplus $50,-000.00, and undivided profits $50,000.00, for a total of $200,000.00, an amount, incidentally, greater than the Rapid City National Bank was originally capitalized for.

I was chairman of the board, Walter Pailing, president; Russell Halvorson, vice president and managing officer. Ed Keating was cashier. A short time later Russell was made president, a position he held until the bank was merged into the American National Bank.

Business started slowly but grew fast in the year and subsequent years. The bank bought loans from us downtown, so in the early days we had more loans than deposits, but the bank was on an earning basis within a short time.

Some time later I was in Washington and called on the Comptroller of the Currency. I thanked him for giving us the charter without delay, and he replied it was no problem because he knew we would run a good bank. Those are nice words coming from the Comptroller.

We have always operated all our banks on the accrual basis, so we know accurately what our earnings and expenses are every day. We accrue daily the amount of interest we have earned, and also accrue daily the amount of interest owing to depositors, and the expenses are estimated for the year and charged daily. Many banks, mostly among the medium size like ours and smaller banks, are on a cash basis. The end result averaged over years will be the same, but you never know exactly how you stand and the exact profit for each year. There is another big advantage in using the accrual system, in that there is a double check and control of the earnings. Twice a year an inventory of the interest due us and the amount due depositors is made up to check against the amount accrued. The difference between the actual interest inventoried and the accrued amounts comes out quite close, and if there is any large difference, then our staff will double-check until they are satisfied there is a good reason for the difference. It is good accounting and prevents the embezzlement or theft of interest due the bank, which can and has happened. A recent news dispatch reported the arrest of a banker in Minnesota for stealing the interest due the bank. With the accrual system, this would be almost impossible.

There were now three institutions in our banking family, all doing well in growth and earnings. At the year end the deposits in the Rapid City National Bank were $21,609,532.63, in the Western National $557,198.-05, and in the Rapid City Trust Company $814,616.54.

34

Nineteen Fifty Seven

This year everything was running very smoothly. After I became chairman of the board, Walter Pailing and the officers were running the bank. I was relieved of the pressure and I was feeling good. I had a little office between the bank and the trust company and I enjoyed visiting with people who came in to see me. I also had more time to think, and perhaps contributed something to the bank and tried to be helpful whenever I could.

One of our problems was that our banking quarters were too small. On some days our lobby was so full that it did not seem there was room for any more people. Our officers were sitting so close that there was no privacy. In our trust company the mortgage activity was so great that there was insufficient room for any more desks and employees. It was fifteen years since we built the building, and we never anticipated that one day it would be too small. We thought of installing an elevator and moving the mortgage and trust department upstairs, but this was not the best solution.

Otto Kepp owned the two lots next to the bank west, and over the past few years I had talked with him about the purchase of the property or perhaps a long-time lease. I was never able to do any business with Otto since he was enjoying a good business in his store. Then one day, out of the clear sky, came Bud Wasser and said Otto had listed the property with him at a price of $100,000.00 Now that was a lot of money and no property had ever sold in Rapid City at such a high price. There was not much choice as far as we were concerned. We needed the property very badly, and if that was his price, I knew Otto too well to argue with him about it. We decided to purchase the property and it was one of the best decisions we have made.

We incorporated the Rapid Building Corporation. The name was later changed to the American Building Corporation. We purchased the property in the new corporation, and also transferred our bank building to the corporation. The corporation was in a position to finance the erection of an addition to our building, doubling it in size. There were perhaps some tax advantages by having at separate corporation own the building.

Now I had something really interesting to do — plan and see that we built a fine building. I found the old drawing board and made several sketches of what I thought we should have. I had taken mechanical drawing in high school and I enjoyed drawing and planning. I had previously made the preliminary sketches of the building we put up fifteen years ago and others when we expanded and remodeled. After much consultation with the officers and directors and we had a general idea of what we wanted, we took the sketches to Frank Moorman, architect, in Minneapolis, a firm that specialized in bank planning and building. Mr. Moorman had been the architect on the original building. I like Frank very much. He is easy to work with. He did not have any fixed idea that architects knew it all and the banker knew

188

nothing. Since he had the plans of the original building, he knew the structure and was well equipped to plan the addition. I think he did a magnificent job blending the two buildings together. It was a big undertaking: preparing the drawings, asking for bids, and then building the building, so it was not until 1960 that it was completed.

We now had 19,954 deposit accounts and 6,956 loans. Our staff had grown to 84. We have been fortunate in that we have always had an efficient staff. They have worked hard, been loyal to the bank, pleasant to work with and have given the bank their best. Perhaps because of the fact that I myself have worked as an employee in every department of the bank, I have been sympathetic to their problems and needs. Once in a while we still have an employee who is a misfit in a bank, but would do better in some other work. Unfortunately, we have the unpleasant duty at times of dismissing an employee. One time we had an employee for one week who we could see was not equipped to be a bank employee, but would make a wonderful receptionist, or she could do some work that would not involve figures, so we dismissed her. We have had employees who were the finest people in the world, but they had no imagination and were slow to comprehend and understand what was expected of them, and we have had to dismiss them. I have always said that the Rapid City National Bank is no place for second-raters. We want our employees to be tops and in that respect we have some of the best in the banking field.

When we have to dismiss employees, we have tried to do it in a way that would not shake their confidence in themselves. We try to explain that they have a place in this world where they can be a success, but we do not think it is in the banking business. We usually give them two weeks' to a month's extra pay to tide them over until they can find another position. In a couple of cases when we dismissed employees who were dependable, but who did not fit into our standards of competence, we offered to keep them on the payroll as long as three months to enable them to find another job. Some people may be failures in one job, but great successes in another.

I have in mind a boy who many years ago left us to become a great success. He was not a failure and except for the talk I had with him, he may still have been with us. I have said that a man or a woman is born to be fast, average or slow. They will never and cannot change gear during their lifetime. This boy was by nature slow, did his work well, but the girls could work rings around him. One day he came to my office and we discussed his future. He was determined to be a banker. I suggested that perhaps he would do better in a small bank where the work was not in as high a gear as at this bank. He took my suggestion, found work in a small bank, transferred later, and is now the president and owner of a small bank in a small town, and I would say a great success. I feel proud of him, and the little talk we had in my office may have been the inspiration he needed.

We carefully check applicants we employ. We want them to be the type that will fit into our organization. We expect them to be neatly dressed. One time we hired a girl on Friday to come to work the next Monday. On Friday she was neatly dressed as an office girl should be. On Monday I hardly recognized her — she came in college clothes, sweater, and saddle shoes. She was out of place, so we had another talk. One day I saw one of our employees with one of those outlandish haystack hair arrangements. I asked Carl Bangert, "Where did you find that girl?" Carl said she did not look like that when he hired her. Our men always wear their coats, and I don't think you have ever seen our men work in shirt sleeves during banking hours. I feel the kind of people we employ reflects the personality and character of the high type bank we operate.

Banks, like people, have a character and a personality.

A bank reflects either warmth or coldness. The way a bank treats people also indicates its character. A smile or a pleasant reception lets customers know they are welcome. Waiting on people quickly, with ease and in a natural manner, reflects that the banker knows what he is doing. In our bank we do not claim to be perfect, but we try hard.

We have always encouraged our officers and employees to purchase stock in this bank when available. Over the years some of our employees, particularly those who have been with us for a long time, have been able to accumulate a considerable amount of bank stock, so that they now have a substantial worth. At the time Roy Dean's estate was settled, there was stock available, and a large number of shares were purchased by the officers of the bank.

A few years ago one of our larger outside stockholders died, and his daughter living in another state far from South Dakota inherited the stock. She came to me and I suggested that inasmuch as she lived so far from Rapid City, she might be interested in diversifying her investment, and we would be interested in buying her stock if she wished to sell. It was a substantial block worth more than $100,000.00. A couple of months later she again appeared in my office and said she had decided to sell, and I made her an offer for the stock. She told me she would be in again, but the next time she came she confided that she had a better offer. I told her that her prospect did not need the stock, that I did not need the stock, nor did I want it for myself. I suggested she look around in our bank at the officers and employees working there. They were the people who had made it possible for me to offer the price I did, and if she sold the stock to me, I would not keep any part of the stock, but give the employees of the bank an opportunity to buy it. She asked if I could offer her a little more so she could refuse the other offer. I said: "How about a dollar more a share?"

She accepted the offer and sold me the stock. I sold the stock to twenty of our officers and employees. I feel I have all the stock I need or want, and I was glad to let my associates, who have had such a big part in building the bank, have the opportunity to accumulate our bank stock.

Since the bank was earning well now and our need to build capital accounts was not of such importance as in the past, the board of directors decided to share some of the earnings with the staff. We set up a profit-sharing fund. This turned out to be a great idea appreciated by the entire staff. The only regret I have is that we did not do it before. We have a liberal plan. Each year we transfer to the profit-sharing fund an amount equal to approximately fifteen per cent of each employee's salary. Since the fund is tax-exempt and there are no income taxes to pay, the fund accumulates rapidly. The fund vests ten per cent per year and after ten years, if an employees leaves, he can take the entire amount to his credit, including all the earnings. If an employee leaves before the ten years, he takes ten per cent of the amount to his credit in the fund for every year he has participated in the fund. If an employee remains with us until retirement, say at sixty-five years of age, the amount in the fund credited to his share can be very substantial. Depending on the salary and the age of the employee, if he is young, it could be over $100,000.00.

In addition, we have a health and accident insurance program which has been of great benefit to many of our employees. In the case of Eugene Pester, who had a long illness before he died, the benefits paid amounted to about $5,000.00. All the premiums are paid by the bank. Each employee is also provided with a life insurance policy, the premium of which is paid by the bank.

For many years we have had a Christmas Party for our staff. The last few years it has been held at the Arrowhead Country Club. Directors, officers, and every employee attend. Husbands bring their wives, and wives bring their husbands. Single persons may bring their boy or girl friends. The last few years we have also invited the officers and staffs of our correspondent banks. It is one great big party and an event looked forward to by everyone.

I have been and am mighty proud of our officers and employees. I feel they are a happy family, intensely loyal to the bank, all working hard to serve our customers well. We have never had any internal politics, jealousies, or squabbles among our staff. They have worked as a team. I feel they have all contributed to the growth of the bank, which would not have been possible without their sincere loyalty and hard work.

Over the years all business firms, and sometimes I think particularly banks, are solicited for donations to various charitable and community projects, all worth while. We have willingly participated. I remember shortly after we opened for business, the late Edward Swander, our director, came in one morning and said: "You are going to be asked to make many donations, and I suggest when you give, you do it cheerfully. If you argue about the merit of the project or do it grudgingly, any good will that could result to the bank will be lost, and you may as well save your money." This was good advice, and we have tried to do just that.

We do not make donations to a church for their annual running expenses, but whenever a church builds a new edifice or educational unit, they are building our community by making it a better place to live, and we have always been glad to contribute to a new church project. On the evening of August 18, 1957, we were visiting friends near Keystone, when we heard on the radio that the large Methodist Church in Rapid City was burning to the ground. The next morning the bank wrote a check for $1,000.00 and sent it to the pastor of the church, together with a letter stating we knew a large and more beautiful church would replace the burned church and wanted to help start their building fund with this donation. The pastor read our letter to the congregation, and the next morning one of our customers came to my desk and said: "I must tell you how proud I was in church yesterday to hear the letter read from MY bank making the first donation to the rebuilding of the church." Perhaps the donations we have made over the years have been a part in building good will for our bank and have made possible our growth.

We have been liberal donators to the United Fund, Red Cross, Hospitals, Churches, YMCA, Student Union at the School of Mines, and most recently to the Boys Club of Rapid City. The total donations made by this bank since organization total $160,778.12, and we feel it has been a good investment in our community.

On November 4, the Western National Bank moved into its new quarters in the Baken Park Shopping Center. It is a very nice building leased from the Center, with a beautiful interior. We added our second Time-Temperature sign to identify the bank. Many people living in the western part of Rapid City found this new bank a great convenience. Deposits doubled during the year. The bank was operating profitably and the surplus fund was increased to $100,000.00. The bank had a drive-in window, and later we added a second one.

The Rapid City Trust Company was also doing well. The surplus fund was increased to $100,000.00 and the total capital funds amounted to $214,160.90 compared to $120,000.00 paid in when the trust company was organized five years before.

The deposits at the year end were $22,231,058.76 in the bank; $1,471,108.64 at the Western; and $1,092,834.-91 in the trust company, representing an increase in all three banks of $2,831,645.70 for the year.

35

Nineteen Fifty Eight

The board of directors up to this time had consisted of five men, all active within the bank, a small board compared to most banks. The examiners suggested from time to time that we should have some outside directors, but it was not a critical suggestion. So this year we thought perhaps it would be a good idea. Outside directors could be very helpful and bring to the bank an outside viewpoint.

Among the men who came to mind was Ivan Landstrom. Ivan moved to Rapid City in 1945 and on borrowed money started a small jewelry store. This grew and he extended his affairs into other enterprises, including the manufacture of the famous Black Hills Gold jewelry. He also formed the Black Hills Glass and Mirror Company. He had proved himself to be a very successful businessman and we felt he could contribute something to the bank as a director. He had been a loyal customer for many years, which was also a consideration.

Another man whose name occurred to us was C. G. Skartvedt. "Skarty," as we affectionately called him, came to Rapid City about the year the bank opened, and no one had been more loyal to the bank giving us all his business. He, too, came to Rapid City with very little money, but being the good businessman he is, he built up extensive oil interests in Rapid City and this area. The board knew he could also contribute materially to the bank from his experience as a solid businessman.

Also coming to mind was B. J. Roskos. Here was a younger man who had lived in Rapid City all his life, had an extensive acquaintance, was a good customer of the bank, and was a self-made man. He is a partner in James Motor Company and had proved himself to be a capable businessman with sound judgment. We felt he could contribute something to the bank that would be valuable.

So at the annual meeting these men were elected to the board of directors. We were happy to have them on our board. They have all been intensely interested and have taken their positions seriously, contributing much to the continued growth of the bank.

Come to think of it, every director and officer of this bank is a self-made man. Not a single one has benefited by an inheritance.

It was in the summer that Ed Gronert, of the Tri-State Milling Company, invited me to go with him to the Republican Convention in San Francisco. I had never been to a political convention before, and looked forward to an enjoyable trip, which it was. We spent about ten days in San Francisco. Ed, as a delegate, was furnished a free car and a chauffeur, and we had a chance to see and become acquainted with the area. I did not stay at the headquarters hotel, but I was at the Mark Hopkins. In the mornings I would have a quiet breakfast in their fine dining room, and having no one to talk to, usually took with me the Wall Street Journal to read.

It was while I was sitting there having my breakfast that I came to the conclusion that interest rates were going to rise. I thought about the three million dollars we had invested in FHA and GI loans. The interest rate at the time was four and one-half per cent on the loans, and any rise in interest rates would substantially increase the discount at which the mortgages could be sold. I decided then and there that the first thing to do upon returning home would be to sell all our mortgages before the price went down. I told Earl Keller, vice president, who was in charge of the mortgage department, to get busy fast and sell all the mortgages, and if necessary obtain additional help. Selling mortgages involves much work with assignments, duplicate records for our file, and necessary paper work. We sold over two and a half million dollars in mortgages within a short time, and as expected, interest rates rose, and the rates on FHA and GI loans rose to five and a quarter per cent. The price on the FHA and GI loans we had sold dropped to about ninety-two cents on the dollar. We saved over $100,000.-00 which we would have lost if we had waited to sell. It was one of the most profitable trips I have made. It is possible I might have reached the same conclusion if I had remained at home, but when I am away from the bank I often have more time to think, so I do not know.

During my banking career in Rapid City I have visited many banks all over the country and talked to many bankers. I have found that such visits have been profitable and have broadened my knowledge of banking matters and problems. I may hear of the experience of other bankers in certain matters, which at the time may not seem important, but later I may have the same problem, and recollect the information stored in my mind. We may hear of the experience of other bankers on loans and other matters which make us better bankers. I have picked up many ideas in bank promotion and advertising. I am sure visits with other bankers have made us better bankers.

The deposits at the year-end were: Rapid City National Bank $26,255,078.43, Western National Bank, $2,251,790.60, and the Rapid City Trust Company $1,238,233.87, for a grand total of $29,745,102.90.

36

Nineteen Fifty Nine

Construction and home building were booming in Rapid City this year. During the year we made $7,701,-674.00 in FHA, GI and First Mortgage loans, a figure we have not equalled since. Our mortgage department was big business, and we made more loans than any other bank, savings and loan association, or mortgage company in South Dakota. We sold most of the mortgages to other investors as there was not enough mortgage money in Rapid City to take care of the demand for such loans.

We sold loans to banks, insurance companies, pension funds, the Commisioner of School and Public Lands in South Dakota, and when the market was tight, to the Federal National Mortgage Loan Association in Chicago. We retained the servicing. The borrower continued to make payments to us. The mortgage department became a very profitable department in the trust company.

Our building expansion was in full swing throughout the year. It was taking longer than expected. Then during much of the construction we had the mess of tearing out and moving around so the workmen could work.

During the construction of the building we hit upon a new idea. Instead of building an unsightly wooden fence in front of the building for people to walk around, we obtained the services or an artist to design a ship to serve as the guard fence. You may enjoy looking at it in the picture section. On the fore part of the ship we had the words: S. S. RAPID CITY NATIONAL as the name of the ship. Underneath were the words: 1st launched in 1941, 2nd launching 1959. The ship's captain was Walter W. Pailing. Then we listed the name of the architect, the contractor and the sub-contractors. On the back part, but not seen on the picture, we listed the names of all the directors under the title "At the Captain's Table." Below, under the name Ship's Crew, we listed all the employees of the bank. It was a grand idea and received much favorable comment.

This year I became interested in the branch bank law of South Dakota, with the possibility of opening a branch in the northeastern part of Rapid City. It was the opinion of the Comptroller of the Currency, the State Banking Commission, and bankers generally that a branch bank could not be opened within the city of the parent bank, although we did have state-wide branching in South Dakota. Upon reading the law on the subject, I discovered it prohibited branching into a city of less than 3,000 population if there was one bank or branch there. Likewise in cities with population of 3,000 to 15,000 people a branch could not be established if there were two banks or branches in the city. In cities of more than 15,000 population there did not seem to be any prohibition to establish an in-city branch, notwithstanding the erroneous interpretation of bankers and supervisory authorities.

We realized we would have to have an opinion from the Attorney General of South Dakota. Mr. Skartvedt suggested a local attorney we could employ to work with the Attorney General for his opinion. The attorney, after researching the law, also came up with an opinion that branching within a city of more than 15,000 population was legal.

I talked to Chief National Bank Examiner Cy Upham in Minneapolis about opening the Northeast Branch in Rapid City. I also talked with him at the State Bankers Association Convention in Sioux Falls, and also talked with Richard Curtis, National Bank Examiner, about the branch. They suggested I should make application.

I should have acted quickly, but with the construction of the addition to our bank I neglected to do so. One day in July I received a jolt when I was informed someone had leaked my thinking about a branch to our competition. It did not take me long to act. I was on a plane for Washington the same day, flying most of the night, and I was in the office of the Comptroller of the Currency the next morning. My first conference was with L. A. Jennings, then First Deputy Comptroller of the Currency. He was of the opinion that we could not open a branch in Rapid City, but stated he was not an attorney, and asked me to come back in the afternoon for a conference with G. W. Garwood, Deputy Comptroller of the Currency, and with their legal counsel.

I had made a short brief of the South Dakota branch banking laws as we interpreted it. The Chief Counsel looked at the brief for a short while and then said: "I think Mr. Dahl is right." Then Mr. Garwood said that in fairness to me he should tell me their office had received two applications for branches in Rapid City from our competitor bank. So I was right — the news had leaked. I said it should make no difference, the idea was mine and I had two conferences with Mr. Upham about it. He asked for those dates and wrote them down on a slip of paper and indicated to me we had not forfeited our priority rights. They asked that we obtain a written opinion from our attorney.

Upon returning home, Mr. Skartvedt and I went to the attorney we had employed and asked for the opinion which he agreed to write. Then I asked him, should we have any trouble, whether he would take care of it for our bank. No, he said, he had been employed by our competitor bank and could not do any further work for our bank, although we had employed him first. I was never so angry in all my life. Here we had employed an attorney in good faith, and then in the middle of the stream he takes employment from our competitor. I think this is the rawest deal I have ever had with an attorney, and the proof of his knowledge that he was wrong is that he never did send us a bill for his services.

We were later asked to obtain an opinion from the Attorney General of South Dakota, which we did. The opinion upheld our contention that branches in cities of more than 15,000 were legal.

Mr. Ray M. Gidney was Comptroller of the Currency at that time. I have seen him on several occasions since, and he always says something like this: "Oh, here is the man who smoked out the branch bank law in South Dakota." He is now chairman of the board of the Florida National Bank in Jacksonville, Florida.

Shades of the past. I came down to work one morning feeling good. I sat down at my desk in my small office and picked up the Independent Banker, a publication of the Independent Bankers Association. Thumbing through the pages, I was startled to find a letter written by O. D. Hanson to Senator Case, and published in the paper. I thought I had had enough trouble with Mr. Hanson when he was on the banking commission in the Rapid City Trust Company matter. Here is the letter in full:

Senator Francis Case
Senate Office Building
Washington, D. C.

Dear Senator Case:

It has been two years now since I completed six years of service on the South Dakota State Banking Commission. While not actually concerned with charter matters officially, I am, nonetheless, interested and very much concerned about the preservation of the dual banking system and about the welfare of the state banks in general, especially in South Dakota.

A situation is developing in Rapid City, South Dakota, now a city of 38,000, that I think is extremely bad. I would like to recall that until 1952, Rapid City had just two banks, both national, the one, as you know, being the Rapid City National, the other the First National Bank of the Black Hills. At that time we granted permission for the Rushmore State Bank at Hill City to move its charter and location to Rapid City. I know you are familiar with this. It is located on St. Joseph at East Boulevard.

In 1952, also, the Rapid City Trust Company adjacent to and controlled by the Rapid City National Bank was established. The Commission at this time felt that there should be no further bank charters granted by the State Banking Department but we yielded to the Rapid City National under a provision whereby they were to operate only as a trust company, divesting themselves of all commercial banking activities.

Following the granting of this charter, there was what seemed to me to be a convenient arrangement whereby a stockholder sued the management, claiming that it had no right to restrict its operations. The one dissatisfied stockholder won and there is now another full fledged bank.

About 1954, a branch of the First National was established at Ellsworth Air Force Base just outside Rapid City.

In 1956, the Western National was chartered by the Rapid City National with a new bank in the vicinity of Harter Addition in Rapid City. This gives the Rapid City area six banking outlets where there were two seven years ago.

At the present time, there is pending before the Comptroller's office the applications of two new branch bank locations, one by the National Bank of the Black Hills, the other by the Rapid City National, both of these are near the location of the Rushmore State Bank.

At the time when Ray Gidney became Comptroller of the Currency, the feeling among state banks throughout the nation was quite generally one of apprehension because it had been, and is, felt that his interest is in the national banking system, and that he has little or no concern for the future of state banks. I have information from what seems a reliable source that it is likely that these two additional bank outlets will be approved by the Comptroller's office. If this is done, I personally will need no further proof that he is indeed not interested in state banks except to eliminate them entirely from the scene.

The Rushmore State Bank experienced, as most new banks do, several years when earnings were low and operating costs comparatively high, and capital gains from earnings were quite small. However, during the past two or three years, it has developed a very good earning position and is now consistently retaining capital earnings from the strengthening of the institution and the protection of its depositors. If these additional charters are granted, it would be extremely difficult to convince any state banker in South Dakota that the Comptroller's office is not perfectly willing to aid existing national banks in eliminating state banks in this state.

Senator Case, I firmly believe that if the Comptroller should go along with a deal of this kind, he is abusing his authority as an appointee of the Federal Government because this action would eminently endanger the existence of a state chartered bank and would seem to be a revival of the days just before World War I when bank charters were issued in our state as promiscuously almost as filling stations and grocery stores.

It is hard for any small bank operator in a town like Rapid City to understand why a large competitor should have four banks blanketing the city where only one existed just six or seven years ago.

A diagram of Rapid City showing present and proposed bank sites is enclosed for your file.

O. D. HANSEN

President
The Bank of Union County
Elk Point, South Dakota

I immediately wrote Mr. Hanson as follows:

THE RAPID CITY NATIONAL BANK
Rapid City, South Dakota
November 13, 1959
Mr. O. D. Hanson, President
Bank of Union County
Elk Point, South Dakota
Dear O. D.:

There is no bank in South Dakota so far distant from Rapid City as your bank in Elk Point, yet I read in the Independent Banker your letter to Senator Case, critical of the Rapid City banking facilities.

The First National Bank of the Black Hills has nine branches, the Rushmore State Bank, one branch, and you yourself have two branches. The Rapid City National has no branches, not even one branch. Don't you think we are entitled to at least one branch?

The Western National was capitalized the same as any other independent bank and operates as such. The Rapid City Trust Company is housed in the same building with the Rapid City National Bank, and is not doing business as a commercial bank and cannot be classified as such.

That leaves four commercial banks in Rapid City. The Villa Ranchaero branch is ten miles east of Rapid City. They serve a community the same as your branch serves Jefferson community. If you want to include this branch, you must also include the population it serves and that makes the picture here even better for another branch.

You say Rapid City has a population of 38,-000 people. The latest survey by the Rapid City Journal gives the Rapid City population to be 45,416, all within the city limits. If you add the population outside the city limits, but exclude the air base, you will find we have a population of greater Rapid City of about 50,000 people.

The population of South Dakota is 704,000 people. There are 224 banking units in South Dakota, or one banking facility for each 3,142 people. Rapid City has one bank for each 12,500 of population. Comparatively speaking we have less banks per population than the state as a whole.

In applying for this branch we are just trying to serve our customers in the area. To come downtown, our customers have to cross two railroads, and pass six stop lights, and if you have tried to fight traffic in Rapid City, you will see we have an entirely different problem than you have in Elk Point. Furthermore we are serving more customers at our drive-in bank than capacity on many days. We need the branch to serve our customers and divert some of this downtown traffic. We have no intention of harming any other bank. All we ask is we may better serve our own customers who now live in the area.

> Yours very truly,
> A. E. Dahl, Chairman of the Board

I sent a copy of this letter to Senator Case. He replied briefly: "Thank you for sending me a copy of that very interesting letter to Mr. O. D. Hanson."

I never did receive a reply from Mr. Hanson, and as far as I know there was no further opposition to our application for the branch. As I said before, Mr. Hanson is a fine fellow, and I cannot help liking him, but our thinking is far apart.

Now that the name of the Independent Bankers Association has been brought up, I am going to make some observations, and I am sure some of my banking friends may not agree with me. We have been a member of the Independent Bankers Association from the time it was organized about thirty years ago. I am confused as to their definition of an "Independent Bank." Their policy has been to fight the establishment of holding companies and branches, particularly in non-branch states, although many of their members have a large number of branches.

The membership includes some very large banks including a large bank in Detroit, a half billion dollar institution, operating twenty-nine branches, yet the association strongly opposes the banks in Minnesota who would like to have even one branch.

The association fought hard against a small banker in Nebraska who sought to establish a holding company in Nebraska, yet they have as a member of the association a bank in Minneapolis that is a member of a registered holding company. They call themselves: Strong Friend of the Independent Banker." Where is the consistency? These are some of the things I do not understand.

We heard nothing further about our branch application this year, but the good news came the following year.

Competition makes life interesting, and I have always liked good competition. Walter Johnson, Robert Driscoll and John Ryan were all good competitors, but best of all, they were socially friendly, and we could always meet and have a nice time together. It was this year that John Ryan retired, and the new management took over at our competitor bank. One day B. J. Roskos, one of our directors, came in to tell me he had heard we were going to have some real competition now. That was fine with me. I know I can think as fast as they, and can, because of our organization set-up, act twice as fast.

Before the year closed we paid another stock dividend, our sixth, amounting to $200,000.00, raising the capital of the bank to $800,000.00. The surplus was increased by the same amount.

On the year-end we had $26,732,993.65 in deposits at the Rapid City National Bank, $2,651,695.98 in the Western National, and $1,281,343.61 in the Rapid City Trust Company.

37

Nineteen Sixty

On January 8, 1960, which was on a Friday, we received a letter from the Comptroller of the Currency giving us authority to open the Northeast Branch of the Rapid City National Bank. I am sure the First National Bank of the Black Hills received the authority to open the Robbinsdale branch in the south part of town the same day. We did not release the information to the press. The First National did, and the following news item appeared in the Rapid City Daily Journal on the ninth day of January. The news was also released by the Associated Press and appeared in many papers in the state: Here it is copied from the Rapid City Daily Journal:

FIRST NATIONAL ANNOUNCES NEW BRANCH

The First National Bank of the Black Hills will soon start construction of a new branch bank building at 1901 Fifth St., Executive Vice President Harold R. Horlocker announced today. According to present plans the new branch will open for business within nintey days - - - -

Banker friends of mine were puzzled and called me on the telephone and asked, "How come? We thought you were the one who applied for a branch." I answered, "We have one, but wait another day and you will hear about it." We were busy, and on Saturday we found a trailer and had it pulled onto the lot we had purchased. We had the sign painters working Sunday to paint us a large sign: Northeast Branch, The Rapid City National Bank. On Tuesday morning we were open for business, and announced that day in the newspapers and on TV and radio that we had a branch open for business. I quote from the news item in the Rapid City Daily Journal on Tuesday, January 12:

NORTHEAST BRANCH BANK OPEN NOW

Temporarily housed in a trailer, Rapid City's newest bank opened for business Tuesday morning at the corner of North Street and Milwaukee Avenue.

The Northeast Branch of the Rapid City National Bank was charted and a certificate to open for business was received Monday.

Bank officials said a permanent brick building will be constructed at the site as soon as possible. Bids on the building will be opened January 28th.

The branch will be under the management of Phil Schroeder, who has been with the bank several years.

The bank announcement said the new facility will have drive-in windows and will render every bank service. A time-temperature sign also will be erected to identify the new branch with the Rapid City National Bank and its affiliated bank, Western National Bank.

The site was chosen to serve banking customers in northeast Rapid City. The branch also will relieve congestion at the downtown drive-in bank, officials said.

The announcement of our opening really started things moving up the street at the bank of our competitor. Overnight they purchased the stock of groceries in the building they were to occupy, and in about three days they were open for business, instead of waiting three months, as stated in the report given to the press a few days earlier. They had so many groceries that they gave them away as door prizes.

In February I received a presidential appointment from President Dwight Eisenhower to serve on the Assay Commission to make the annual inspection at the U.S. Mint in Philadelphia. This was a nice honor. I accepted and met at the mint together with eleven other appointees. It seems the Assay Commission was established about the time of the founding of our country, for the purpose of having civilians make a check on the coins minted. We were divided into three groups. One was to count samples of coins taken at random from the mints. Another group weighed the coins to see that they had the proper weight. The last group watched a certain number of coins melted down to see that they had the proper silver content. The work took one day and we were all rewarded with a specially cast medallion of the commission with the year and date. Also on my wall in the office I have an impressive certificate, complete with the gold Presidential seal and the President's signature. It was a pleasant experience and an honor I appreciated.

We were coming along nicely with the new building. The blank wall behind the tellers looked like a suitable place for a mural. I had seen a beautiful historic mural in the Bank of Sheridan, Wyoming, many years before. Ivan Landstrom and I flew in his private plane to Sheridan. We were fortunate that the artist, Bernard Thomas, who now lives in Florida, was home on his vacation. Ivan and I made a deal then and there for Mr. Thomas to paint a historic mural for us. He came to Rapid City and spent some time researching this area, bought himself some books on the Black Hills, and departed for his home in Florida. He returned about three months later and went to work.

Mr. Thomas has had an interesting career. Born at Sheridan, the seventh son of the seventh son, he attended the University of Minnesota. Later he attended Woodbury College in Los Angeles, where he won the Leo Youngsworth award as the outstanding senior art student. During the war Thomas was an infantry sergeant in the European theater. He gained national recognition for his painting "For Thou Art With Me," created for the Chaplain Division. General George Patton was so impressed by his work that his headquarters provided him an art scholarship in the Ecole de Beaux Arts studio in Paris.

After returning from the war, Thomas painted for the noted opera singer, James Melton, at his Autorama in Hypoluxo, Florida, the largest three-dimensional mural in the world painted by one man, illustrating chronologically American history from the landing of the Pilgrims to the San Francisco Fire. I had an opportunity to see this mural and enjoy its outstanding beauty.

The painting of the mural in the bank created unusual interest on the part of the customers who came to see him work. Mr. Thomas is a large man, has large hands, and he usually worked in western clothes with cowboy boots. He perhaps did not look like an artist, but he has outstanding talent. We purchased TV time, and he appeared several times with guests explaining the mural.

We had a contest to name the mural which brought a larger number of entries. The contest was won by Sister Joseph Ann, O.S.B., St. Martin's Academy, Sturgis,

with the slogan OVER THE HORIZONS OF YESTER-
DAY — INTO OUR HERITAGE OF TOMORROW.

The mural is eighty feet long and seven feet high. It
is one of the most beautiful historic murals painted, and
we are mighty proud to have it in our bank. The lower
section has many interesting features and emphasizes the
four seasons of the year. At the far left you will see the
budding trees blending into the foliage of spring. In the
center section you see summer with the hills around the
city turning brown. Further right you see the golden
colors of fall. At the extreme left are the snows of winter.

Again to the left, the first section portrays the rec-
reational area of the Black Hills. Here you see Harney
Peak, the highest peak east of the Rockies. The famous
Mount Rushmore memorial is only a white spot on the
mountain, but the artist has lifted an enlarged portion
into the skies so you may see its real beauty. The center of
the mural indicates the location of Rapid City exposing
the gateway to the Black Hills, with a composite of industrial, commercial, and civic buildings making up the
foreground. There are groups of people standing in two
places, representing typically the people of the area. Cattle, farm scenes, jet bombers, bad lands, and other true-
to-life objects and scenes are on the mural.

The upper portion depicts past history. There are
shown dinosaurs and other animals that once roamed
over the area. There are early Indians, trappers and ex-
plorers. In the center over Rapid City are the founders
of Rapid City. Shown are prospectors working a gulch
for gold. Historic scenes include an early train, a stage
coach, a Rapid City street, cattle herds, and other things
of interest.

When the artist first showed me the sketch of the
proposed mural, I was surprised to find he had included
my picture on the mural. I am standing near life size behind four other men representing the industry of the

community. The artist explained I was to represent the business man and banker backing the community. I think some of the officers, including Frances Vincent, had a part in making my picture part of the mural. Naturally I was flattered and since the artist placed me in the background so I did not stick out like a sore thumb, I made no objection. The mural and bank will be here long after I am gone, so perhaps the future generations can look at the guy with glasses who was present the day the bank opened for business, and remained around for many years, and perhaps had a part in the growth of the bank.

The mural was featured in the Picture Section in the Minneapolis Sunday Tribune. We had nearly a thousand requests for our booklet in color and a description of the mural and history of the artist. It is one of the tourist attractions in Rapid City. Best of all, the mural gives a warm feeling in our attractive bank lobby. It was one of the best investments we have made. Readers of this book may have a brochure in color describing the mural free for the asking by writing to the bank.

In April the construction of our new building was completed. On the right side of the building we have a large customers' lobby. Featured are individual check desks. On the left is a large officers' section. The trust department uses the back part of the building with separate outside entrance. A large directors' room is also in the rear part of the building. A large part of the basement is used by our bookkeeping department. Carpets and drapes with a sea of light from the ceiling add much to the warm, friendly atmosphere of the building. I have traveled much and have seen many bank buildings, but when I return home, I feel we have one of the finest and friendliest banking quarters in the country.

On Sunday, April 24, we had Visitation Day, different from any grand openings I have heard of. We had an experience when we remodeled our first banking quar-

213

Construction of Addition

Completed 1960

Bank Lobby

Officers' Section

Mural

ters nearly twenty-five years ago. Customers had seen the work in progress during the remodeling, so when we had open house, few people came. The same thing was true in our present remodeling, since most people had seen the work in progress. So we thought we should have something different, if we were to have people come.

We decided to give Dollars to the Churches. We gave all adult visitors a coupon worth a dollar to the church of their choice. They could deposit the coupon in the church collection plate, and we would redeem each coupon with a dollar. It was an original idea with us. We had never heard of any bank using this idea, but a few banks have since used Dollars for Churches. One bank in Connecticut used it with great success.

We decided to have Visitation Day on Sunday. We had open house from one o'clock in the afternoon to eight o'clock in the evening. Thousands came, and about two o'clock the bank was so full of people that we hardly had room for them. By actual count we had 9,218 visitors, of whom 7,046 were adults who received certificates, and 2,172 were junior citizens. When you read of openings with 15,000 to 25,000 attending, I don't believe it. We had all we could do to handle 9,000 people.

How many banks have had their openings announced from the pulpits and have had the opening printed in their church bulletins? We did. We know the seven thousand dollars we donated to the churches was money well spent and brought us much good will. Visitation Day was a great success for us.

An innovation for us upon the opening of our new building was the employment of a full-time receptionist. We have a very personable lady at a desk just inside the front door to greet our customers, help them find the officer they wish to see, and also direct them to where the service desired is performed. She answers many questions about the bank and spends much of her time in the lobby visiting with people. If anyone is interested in the mural, she will tell them about it and explain the many interesting features. It is just one idea to make people feel at home in our bank, and we have had many compliments from the public about our receptionist and the service she has performed.

It was in the early part of the year that I was at the Hilton Hotel in Los Angeles one day preparing to go down for breakfast. The telephone rang and it was Walter Pailing, president of our bank. He told me Chris Hogan, our customer and owner of Rapid Chevrolet, had just been in the bank and told him he had been offered a directorship at the First National Bank of the Black Hills. The breakfast did not taste so good.

Chris had been a valuable customer of our bank for many years and did all of his business with us. It seemed rather peculiar they should select one of our customers to be a director. They certainly had many qualified men who were customers of their bank, and need not invite one of our customers. It has always been our policy to think of our own customers first.

Chris Hogan came in to see me upon my return. He felt bad about leaving us and taking his business with him but he did feel it was an honor he could not refuse. We had a very friendly visit and I did not try to talk him out of it, and I certainly did not blame him for wanting to take the directorship. Chris has always been a good friend of mine and continues to be.

I also learned upon returning to the bank that they had invited another customer to become a director in their bank. He was a prominent man representing one of the business firms in Rapid City. After discussing the matter with Walter Pailing, he decided he enjoyed doing business with us and refused the offer.

I was at my desk in the bank the next Saturday afternoon when about four o'clock the telephone rang. Another customer, a prominent business man, called and wanted to come to the bank and see me. I told him to come, and when he walked in the door to my office, I said to him: "I know why you are here — you have been offered a directorship at the First National Bank of the Black Hills." It was pure guess on my part, and he was surprised and asked: "How did you know?" Well, I told him they had been passing out directorships to our customers, as if the only capable men in town were our customers, and they did not have any customers worthy of these positions. We had a friendly visit and he was inclined to accept, but something must have happened. I don't know, but I believe they stirred up a protest from their own customers. The offer was withdrawn and they found two of their own customers qualified to be directors.

By this time it was getting under my skin, so foolishly or not, I wrote to John Sweeney, vice president of the Northwest Bancorporation, owner of the First National Bank of the Black Hills, in part as follows: "It would be a surprise to me if the tactics of your people here are those of the corporation. I think it has been said that the holding company banks are ethical and honorable competitors and that has been my belief. I personally have been friendly with many of the group bankers, but I have never before heard of the methods used here. Yet, if these men were added to the board, it will require a special stockholders' meeting and a new resolution to increase the board, and it is in your power to either approve or disapprove these tactics."

I never did receive a reply, so the Bancorporation must have approved. I thought to myself that if that is the way the competition wanted to play, we would take some of their deposits. We had been asked to open a branch in Hot Springs, but we never did, preferring to confine ourselves to Rapid City. A few days later, Henry Freed and R. W. Coleman, both from the Midwest Furniture store in Hot Springs, walked in. I invited them into my office and asked how they would like to have a branch from our bank in Hot Springs. They were delighted and arranged for a meeting with the businessmen in Hot Springs for me. I thought that if the First National was going to raid our customers with directorships, we would go to Hot Springs where they have a branch and take a million dollars of their deposits. I am sure it has worked that way, and they would now have at least that much more in deposits if we had not opened the branch.

I had a friendly meeting with the businessmen in Hot Springs and they were enthusiastic about our coming to their city. We filed an application for the branch. That is how we got into the branch banking outside of Rapid City. If the above incidents had not happened, we may never have had this branch.

The application was approved and we opened for business on October 24, 1960. We bought a building across from the Post Office. We remodeled it beautifully with the new type staggered tellers' windows. We had a grand opening and again gave Dollars to Churches. The branch has been a success, and today we have about three million dollars in deposits in this branch. According- ing to a Federal Reserve Bank report on bank debits, we have forty per cent of the volume in Hot Springs at the present time. We have been pleased with our reception there.

There was a legal question involved. We crossed one county, and Hot Springs is sixty miles from Rapid City. The state banking commission had passed a rule we could not cross another county and no branch could be more than fifty miles from the parent bank. We secured an opinion from our attorney, and it was his opinion this rule does not apply to National banks. We heard no objection from the banking commission.

Two years later the National Bank of South Dakota merged three banks more than fifty miles from the home office in Sioux Falls. This time the banking department through the Attorney General brought suit pleading they

219

had violated the South Dakota branch bank law. We were much interested in the outcome of the lawsuit, because if the banking department won, we also would be forced to close the branch at Hot Springs, or incorporate a unit bank to take over the business. The lawsuit was tried both in the state and federal courts, and the banking department again lost on every count. The Supreme Court of South Dakota held that the banking commission had no authority to pass such a rule. In Federal Court it was carried up to the Supreme Court in Washington, and the banking department lost the second time.

I have always enjoyed traveling and visiting other cities and countries. It had been my ambition since my service in the First World War to go to Europe. This year the opportunity came to go on a tour of Europe with a group of bankers leaving after the American Bankers Association convention in New York. There were fifty-five bankers in the group. Mrs. Dahl and I left New York with the bankers on September 21. The tour lasted about twenty days, and we visited London, Paris, Nice, Genoa, Florence, Rome, Madrid, and Lisbon. It was a delightful trip and we made many acquaintances with bankers we did not know before. Traveling in Europe is easy. The people in hotels, stores, and air terminals all speak English. The cab drivers don't know anything and you had better have your destination written on a piece of paper to be sure you will get to where you want to go.

This year we built and completed a fine small bank building for our Northeast Branch. Here we provide two drive-in windows and a walk-up window. We have plenty of parking for our customers. We installed another Time-Temperature sign to identify this branch.

We had another problem and that was the name of the bank. Now that we were in Hot Springs and in the branch bank business, we did not think it appropriate to have the name Rapid City National Bank in Hot Springs.

I never did like the name too well anyway. All the name suggested was that we were a National bank located in Rapid City. There had always been some confusion in Rapid City because the name was not distinctive in any way. We explored many names, and the directors decided we should change the name of our bank to the American National Bank, which we did. It is a name that could be used in any town, and since there was no such name anywhere in the state, we could use it in any further expansion into other towns. We were well pleased with our new name.

We found that changing the name of the bank cost money. The large name on the front of our main office was changed. The names on our branches and the Time-Temperature signs had to be changed. We had to have some new stationery and certain legal forms changed. We continued to use our deposit slips and as many of our old forms as we could.

The deposits at the year end were: in the American National $28,206,523.52, in the Western National $2,-984,117.88, and in the Rapid City Trust Company $882,-085.68.

38

Nineteen Sixty One

The number of customers using the drive-in bank across the street continued to grow so our facilities were inadequate. This time we decided there would be no further remodeling, but instead we would tear down the old building and build all new facilities. This year we built a new Auto Bank, complete with three drive-in positions for customers in automobiles. We also provided a fine enclosed walk-up lobby with two tellers' windows. It is unique in appearance. We surrounded the lot with masonry screen and beautifully landscaped grounds. We now have the finest Auto Bank in town.

For the Early Birds, the windows open at eight in the morning, and for the Nite Owls, we remain open to five-thirty in the evening, with two extra hours on Friday.

In Rapid City we now have seven drive-in windows, three downtown at the Auto Bank, two at the Western, and two at the Northeast branch. We have four walk-up windows, two downtown, and one each at the Western and the Northeast branch. We also have four After-

Auto Bank Downtown

Directors At Opening Northeast Branch

Automation 1965

Hour depositories — one at the front entrance of our main office, one at the Auto Bank, and one each at the Western and the Northeast branch.

This year we were saddened by the death of **Eugene Pester**, vice president and trust officer, after a long illness. Eugene was a brilliant man. Under his wise direction and supervision the trust company showed a steady growth. Sincerity, loyalty of purpose, and high sense of honor were among his strong assets.

Clark Carnaby, who had been trust officer at the Omaha National Bank for many years, joined the trust company as vice president and trust officer, to take the vacant position.

Business in Rapid City continued to boom. The construction of three Titan missile complexes had much to do with the continued growth. The announcement of the installation of one hundred fifty Minuteman missiles in the area added more fuel to the boom. Construction and home building continued at a rapid pace. Everybody enjoyed good business.

After my trip to Europe I became interested in a Travel Department for the bank. I found it would be difficult to open one from scratch and obtain the appointments from the airlines which are so necessary. We made a deal with the Rowell McDonald Travel Agency to move their agency to the bank. We had a nice space just inside the door which we were not using, and it has been an ideal location for the department. I was very much interested in going to Europe again. The Travel Department arranged a twenty-seven day trip, and I was to be the Tour Director. Thirteen people joined our tour and on September 3 I left with the group. Being a tour director is not so difficult. At every stop we were met by a tour guide for that city. He met us at the airport, helped us through customs, and provided transportation to the hotel where room reservations were ready for us. He guided us on the tours in the city. My biggest job was to see we did not miss anyone, and to count the baggage when we were leaving or arriving in the next city.

We arrived in London the next morning, where we spent four days. We made a trip to the Shakespeare Country and also to Windsor Castle. We then went to Brussels in Belgium, and on to Oslo, Norway. Since my father was born in Moss, Norway, I had an opportunity to visit the city about seventy miles from Oslo. We went on to Stockholm, Sweden, and then to Copenhagen, Denmark. From here we visited Cologne, Wiesbaden, Frankfurt and Heidelberg, all in Germany. We took a steamer ride down the Rhine. We proceeded on to Lucerne, Switzerland, and had a most interesting trip through the Alps. Our next stop was Rome, a most interesting city. Carl Zill, who was in our party, arranged for him and me to attend the Audience with Pope John at his summer home. There was a large group and I was able to take several pictures of the Pope at close range. We then proceeded to Paris, and after three days there left for home.

One of the last days of December, about four o'clock in the afternoon, Harold J. Walker, president of the Bear Butte Valley Bank at Sturgis, called on the telephone. He wanted to see me and wanted to know if he could come down that afternoon. He said he had made up his mind what he wanted to do, and would come soon.

As he sat at my desk he took from his pockets some adding machine lists and on a piece of paper added together the capital, surplus, undivided profits, reserves, and accruals, plus an amount to round out his figures as to the value of the stock in his bank. He said he had decided to sell and wanted to know if we would buy the bank. I told him yes, and said I would see him in the morning.

Mr. Walker is a remarkable man. He had operated the bank in Sturgis for thirty-seven years very successfully, and at the time of the bank troubles in the early thirties he survived the storm, never closed his doors and had no reorganization. He operated the bank carefully, always showing good judgment, and he had a reputation as an outstanding banker. He had the confidence of the community.

I had visited with Mr. Walker about a year earlier in his bank. He invited me into the back room to his desk and showed me some figures of accomplishment and earnings over the period he had operated the bank. He then asked me if I would buy the bank. I did not take him seriously, so I told him: "You know good and well we would be willing to buy your bank, Harold, but I will never ask you, because I know you do not want to sell." That ended the conversation, and I was surprised when he came in and offered to sell the bank.

After Mr. Walker's departure I visited with some of the other directors, but we did not agree as to how the stock would be split. I had a feeling the two largest stockholders in our bank had enough stock, and that it would be advantageous for our profit-sharing fund to have a big block of stock so all our employees would have an interest in the bank. The officers should have an opportunity to take the stock they wanted and the directors who had a lesser amount should also have a chance to increase their holdings. I also thought of selling a few shares to some of the people in Sturgis and Hot Springs. In making this suggestion, I had in mind that the stock would be exchanged for American National Bank stock upon a merger. Nothing came of the meeting with the directors.

The next morning I first called the First National Bank of Minneapolis stating that I would like to borrow about a half million dollars. R. W. Hanson, executive vice president, agreeably said "Yes" immediately. I then asked Walter Pailing, president, to accompany me and we drove to Sturgis and purchased the bank from Mr.

Walker on a contract settlement immediately after the first of the year.

I did not want any of the stock for myself, but Walter and I continued to hold the stock in our names, representing about eighty per cent of the outstanding stock, pending a possible merger of the bank with the American National Bank, which I will cover in next year's chapter.

Our deposits grew fast this year and business was booming. This seemed to be too good to last and in our annual report at the year-end I wrote:

> Presently we have boom times in Rapid City due in part to the large governmental expenditures for the Titan and Minuteman missile installations. It is a good time to plan carefully and both business and individuals should build to put their affairs in a strong position so they will not be hurt when the boom tapers off. This is what we are doing at our banks.

Our deposits at the year-end in the bank were $34,088,590.51, at the Western $3,742,875.78, and in the trust company $1,036.987.38. The increase for the year was the large amount totaling $6,794,720.89.

39

Nineteen Sixty Two

On January 2, Walter Pailing and I drove to Sturgis and completed the purchase of the Bear Butte Valley Bank. Fred Barth, vice president of our bank, who had been with us nearly thirty years, wanted to go to Sturgis and manage the bank. We happily agreed, and he was elected president.

Mr. Walker asked if we would retain his son Bruce as an officer in the bank. This we agreed to do because we really needed Bruce very much. He had a big following among the ranchers, and since he had handled a large part of the ranch and livestock loans, we wanted him to continue to do so. We immediately promoted him from assistant cashier to vice president with a raise in salary. Bruce is without doubt the most experienced and knowledgeable man in our organization about livestock loans.

The community reacted favorably to our coming to Sturgis. Fred told me it was a sad day the first day he was there. Many of the old timers came to the bank with tears in their eyes to see Mr. Walker, and to think that he had sold the bank that had so faithfully taken care of them for so many years was perhaps a shock. But when they heard that both Harold and Bruce would remain with the bank, they felt better. They soon found we were not going to make any radical changes and they were happy with us. Deposits continued to grow. They also liked Fred, who had considerable experience with livestock loans, as well as commercial, real estate, and other loans.

We immediately made application to the Comptroller of Currency to merge the bank with the American National Bank. We soon found the preparation of a merger application was no small task. The application consisted of thirty-four pages and eleven copies were required. The application contained copies of the agreement to purchase the bank, certified copies of the resolution of the Board of Directors of both banks to merge; agreement of consolidation; financial history of both banks; statement of assets and liabilities and consolidated figures; description and explanation of adjustments. There were also schedules of adequacy of capital structure, future earnings prospects, and management. We supplied maps of the area, located competing banks and branches. We covered lending power and new services to be offered in the branch. We had to include all competition, including savings and loan associations. We made an analysis of duplicate loans and discounts, service charges, and interest rates. Filing a merger application involves much work but is an interesting experience.

We included an index, mimeographed every page, and printed an attractive cover. It was a well-prepared application and we were complimented by the supervisory authorities on the complete and the nice manner in which the application was presented.

The application for merger was approved, and on May 1, 1962, the two banks merged. The Bear Butte

Valley Bank became the Bear Butte Valley branch of the American National Bank.

After Walter Pailing and I received American National Bank stock for the stock we held in the Bear Butte Valley Bank, we sold the shares as outlined above and repaid our loan. Walter retained some of the stock, but I sold all I had acquired, and ended with no additional investment. Neither Walter nor I made any money out of the transaction. My sole purpose was to acquire the bank for the benefit of all the stockholders of the American National Bank and not to make money, which I could have done.

On June 27, 1962, Oscar Brosz, Superintendent of Banks for South Dakota, wrote us that we should have converted the Bear Butte Bank to a national bank before the merger. This bank is supervised by the Comptroller of Currency in Washington, and the State Superintendent of Banks and the Banking Commission in South Dakota should have nothing to say in the matter. I thought our troubles with the South Dakota banking department were over after the Rapid City Trust Company matter was settled, but here we are again.

I flew to Pierre for a conference with Mr. Brosz. He dropped the matter of conversion to a national bank, because in this matter he was entirely wrong. He now brought up another point. He quoted to me from the South Dakota Code that the Sturgis bank should publish official notice that the bank was in liquidation. That was impossible, because after a merger, the bank becomes a part of the surviving institution, and in effect is not in liquidation. I also pointed out to him that there were several state banks in South Dakota that have in the past been merged with national banks, and not one of these banks had published liquidation notices, so why was he picking on us? It was suggested I should meet with the Banking Commission.

Again I flew to Pierre. I did not get any further with

the commission. One of the commissioners said that just because something had been done wrong in the past was no reason to repeat the error now. Mr. Brosz said he needed the liquidation notice to close his records on the Sturgis bank. I pointed out that the Certificate of Merger issued by the Comptroller of the Currency should be sufficient. I departed.

We took the matter up with our attorney who researched the law on the subject and wrote his opinion upholding our contention. He also flew to Pierre and presented the matter to the Attorney General, and that was the last we heard. The cost to us of the opinion and the three trips to Pierre amounted to over $400.00, all for no purpose.

After completing this merger we began thinking about merging the Western National Bank and the Rapid City Trust Company into the American National Bank. It was now possible to make the Western a branch, which we did not know at the time it was chartered as a separate bank. The Rapid City Trust Company would become the trust department of the American National Bank. There would be several advantages and some saving by having only one bank. So we made a second application to effect this merger, and on September 1, 1962, the three institutions were merged into one bank. We made a slight change in the name of the bank by adding the words "and Trust Company" to our title.

There were some advantages to our customers. In Rapid City we maintain one set of books for all our three offices. This means our customers may use the office most convenient to them, and use another office the next day if they so desire. There is no mix-up as to which office the check is drawn on. In Sturgis and Hot Springs we maintain separate books.

The merger of the Bear Butte Valley Bank added $531,841.89 to our capital funds. The Western National contributed $296,897.81 to capital funds and $51,118.36

to Reserve for Losses. The Rapid City Trust Company provided $266,691.64 in capital, surplus and profits to the American National Bank, and $14,800.00 to Reserve for Losses.

We ended up with an odd amount of capital stock outstanding totaling $1,170,000.00, so we decided to declare another stock dividend of $230,000.00, increasing our capital stock to $1,400,000.00. We also increased the surplus fund to the same amount.

It may be interesting to note that in the six years the Western National Bank operated as a separate institution, and after the payment of $32,000.00 in dividends, the capital funds increased from $200,000.00 paid in on organization to $296,896.81 at the time of the merger. In addition, the bank had built up a Reserve for Losses account of $51,118.13, for a grand total of $348,016.17.

The Rapid City Trust Company did even better because it had the income from the profitable mortgage department. The Trust Company had operated for ten years, a longer time than Western. The dividends paid amounted to $113,000.00. The capital funds increased from $120,000.00 paid in to $266,691.64 at the time of the merger. In addition, it had set aside $14,800.00 for Reserve for Losses.

Russell Halvorson, who had managed the Western National Bank, decided to return to the main office in the commercial loan department. Jerry Harder was elected manager of the branch.

Agnes and I flew to Minneapolis in July on business and also to visit my mother who had been in bad health the past few years, and we knew she was failing fast. I had not notified my brother Victor we were coming. When later he met us at the airport, he did not have to tell us — we knew mother had passed away. She had passed her eighty-ninth birthday a few days before. She was an example of good Christian living and always an inspiration to all of us. She was a wonderful mother, and we are thankful we could have her with us for so many years. Nevertheless, it left a feeling of sadness in our hearts to part.

I was elected to the Board of Regents of Augustana College in Sioux Falls. This is a very fine institution and the largest private college in the state. Since I did not have the opportunity to go to college, my service on the board will have to be my college education.

Our deposits jumped to $48,522,297.52 on December 31, largely due to the merger with the Bear Butte Valley Bank.

40

Nineteen Sixty Three

This year we became interested in automation. We could see the handwriting on the wall that sooner or later we would also have to convert to compete in a changing world. Many banks of comparable size were purchasing or leasing automation equipment. The changeover, when it came, would be expensive, and it would take a year or two to effect the savings we had to have. We decided we would not rush into automation, and it would be doubtful if we would make the change until our competition also decided to automate. There would be some advantages if we automated about the same time.

I attended an automation conference in Detroit. I will admit much on the agenda was over my head, but I did learn about some ground work and the problems we would have to face. Our officers all took advantage of visiting other banks that were in automation, and we continued to learn about their problems. We found what automation could do for us, and also what it could not do. We also had an opportunity to see the equipment of various manufacturers. The salesmen called on us regularly, and we compared one against the other, and we learned much from them. But automation was not for us this year. We were not in a hurry, and there was little or no advantage to be first to install automation. I fully realize the customers do not care whether we prepare and keep their books on automation equipment, on our present equipment, or even by pen and ink, so long as we do it accurately. So we passed automation this year.

We completed a very beautiful and functional banking house for the Bear Butte Valley Office in Sturgis, at a cost of about a quarter of a million dollars. I told Fred Barth, vice president and manager, one day that it was too much money to spend for a branch building. "Yes," he answered, "but I manage the third largest bank in the Black Hills." How right he was. We had a grand opening and again used Dollars for Churches. We had a large crowd and everybody was pleased.

We now have the most modern banking houses for all our offices. We also have the beautiful Auto-Bank downtown. The American Building Corporation, wholly owned by the bank, owns the buildings and finances their cost. Loans have been made at the First National Bank of Minneapolis on an unsecured basis. The corporation is making money, and using the fast depreciation, the cash flow is good. Since it now looks as if we have come to the end of building our buildings, we can steadily reduce the debt and pay the balance within five years.

The travel bug had bit me. I found traveling in foreign countries easy and enjoyable. This time Mrs. Dahl and I joined a group of bankers and their wives for a trip around the world. We left Washington, D.C., after the convention of the American Bankers Association and flew first to Paris, where we changed planes for a flight to Athens, Greece. We found this city interesting and

Western Branch

Northeast Branch

Sturgis Branch

Hot Springs Branch

of course we had to visit the Acropolis — the ancient ruins of temples, amphitheatres and other buildings, which were built more than 2,000 years ago. So far back into history and without modern building equipment, the people of that era must have had some brilliant architects, engineers, and builders to construct such large and beautiful buildings. The results of their skill, still visible today, are truly amazing.

We proceeded to Beirut, Lebanon. Here is a very modern city on the Mediterranean. Our hotel accommodations were the finest we have seen anywhere. This city is worth a stop on any tour. We flew most of the night to New Delhi, India. From there we drove 125 miles to Agra to see the Taj Mahal, one of the seven wonders of the world, and a most beautiful structure. We also went on to Jaipur, where we had an elephant ride, and I must say it was different, but a highlight of our trip. Returning to New Delhi, we flew to Calcutta, one of the large cities of the world. I do not think I would go to India for a vacation, but I would not have missed seeing it. Here we find poverty at its worst, poorly dressed people, thin and underfed people, naked children, holy cows on the sidewalks and the streets, and people by the thousands sleeping on the sidewalks.

We visited Rangoon, Burma, for two days and then Bangkok, Thailand. The two countries are similar. Most of the people are Buddhists, but without the great poverty in India. We flew to Hong Kong, a very interesting place to visit. Here you may buy cameras and clothing for less money than anywhere else, and it is a great place for women to shop. Most interesting to me was Aberdeen, where thousands of people live on boats. They are born on a boat, live all their lives on a boat, and die on a boat. We also visited the New Territories, and could see Red China a short distance away.

Our last foreign country to visit was Japan. Here the people all work and the country is very prosperous. The

237

women wear western dress on the streets, but the kimonos are used in the home and on festive occasions. We took several side trips in the country and to their resort cities. Buildings are modern and automobiles are everywhere. A trip to Japan is interesting and very much worth while. Flying to Honolulu, we crossed the International Date Line, and after returning home we received a certificate marking the event. From Honolulu we returned to Los Angeles.

There were twenty bankers and our wives in the group. We flew about 25,000 miles without incident. It was the most enjoyable trip we have taken.

I wrote a column every other day entitled AROUND THE WORLD WITH ART DAHL published in the Rapid City Daily Journal. I later had the columns reprinted in a folder. It must have been a good idea, for I received many comments and letters telling me how much they were enjoyed.

We changed our investment policies. For many years we did not purchase municipal bonds. Over the years our growth was so rapid, and our problem was to build capital funds to keep up with the growth. For measuring the adequacy of capital, the Comptroller of the Currency had a yardstick of measuring risk assets to capital funds. Municipal bonds were considered as risk assets the same as loans. Since we had to take care of our loan demand, we did not have any more room for municipal bonds, and have a favorable risk asset ratio to capital funds. Two things have changed. The Comptroller of Currency abandoned the old rule, and now measures the adequacy of capital as to quality of assets, management, occupancy expense, earnings and history of the bank, and in these matters we score favorably. The second reason is that we now have built our capital funds to where we do have a good ratio to both deposits and risk assets. So this year we decided to again invest in municipal bonds, and acquired more than two million dollars in such bonds during the year.

We confine our investments in municipal bonds to state issues and South Dakota municipalities. We will use our municipal bonds for pledge to secure public funds. For that reason we will not need them for liquidity and we have purchased longer term maturities. The tax exempt feature will benefit our earnings in a measurable amount.

I suppose everyone has some pet peeve. Mine is to pick up a telephone, make a call, and be greeted with the reply, "Who's calling?" Or perhaps a little more diplomatic response, "May I say who is calling?" To me it should not make any difference who is calling. It makes me feel that if I am important, the boss will accept the call, otherwise not. Another peeve is answering the telephone and having a secretary tell me: "Mr. Blank wants to talk to you." Now I do not mind if Mr. Blank is ready to talk and does not keep me waiting, but it is not always so. One time not so long ago I had such a call from Chicago. I did not recognize the name, but I had a suspicion it was a bond broker who wanted to sell some bonds. I waited a long time, and after waiting for what I thought was much too long, I banged the receiver on the hook. Soon the call came again, and the voice said: "We were disconnected." I said, "No, I got tired of waiting and thought my time was just as valuable as yours." He apologized, and as I had anticipated, he offered to sell some municipal bonds. I was not in the mood to buy any.

At the American National Bank our operators have strict orders to make the connection to the person called at once. If they ask who is calling, we may have a new operator. Our operators also have orders to put through all telephone calls, even if the officer is in a meeting or a conference. How many times have I been told the person I called was in a conference and could not talk to me. If the officer is in the building, he will be called no matter what he is doing. There might be some valuable business on the other end of the line and we want to be helpful.

Not long ago I called a businessman in Rapid City to make a purchase for one of our branches. The first time I called, I was told he was in a conference. The second time I was greeted with: "Who's calling?" I decided I would call his competitor.

When we remodeled our building we placed the switchboard in the officers' section, where the operator can see all our officers, with the exception of our trust officers in the rear part of the building. She also has a good view of the banking lobby, which could be of some protection. We found this to be a very good plan. The operator can see immediately if the officer is at his desk, and if not, perhaps she can see him in some other part of the bank. I am sure we can give better telephone service to our customers because of the placement of the switchboard.

Perhaps you may think these are trivial matters, but it is the many small things, and just a little better service, that add up to big things, and they have all had a part in our growth.

This year we declared our eighth stock dividend of $100,000.00, increasing our capital to $1,500,000.00. The surplus was increased to a like amount.

The deposits at the year-end were $51,635,990.31.

41

Nineteen Sixty Four

With the completion of the Titan and Minuteman installations, we felt a recession during the year, and the boom was over. Bank debits and sales have been running below last year. Building of homes and other construction have been greatly curtailed.

The strength of our economy is diversity of income in the community, much more perhaps than in most communities. Retail sales have held very well, with a large increase in the last quarter. Wholesalers are extending out further in the distribution of their products. The tourist industry had a successful year and we look for an increase in 1965. The mining and lumbering industry had a prosperous year. Livestock prices are lower, but we have had ample rain the past year so the feed situation was ample. We had good crops. The Ellsworth Air Force base continues to hum with activity, and contributes much to our economy. With a pickup in construction, Rapid City will continue to grow.

In the year 1964 we had forty-nine foreclosures on

241

Building New Apartment

mortgages owned or sold to investors. All were on FHA loans with one exception, which was a GI mortgage. We had no foreclosures on conventional loans. At first this may seem like a very large number, but when we consider the total mortgages owned and serviced (we had at the year end 3,014 mortgage loans totaling $30,324,812.-27), the number is relatively small. During the history of the bank we have had 79 foreclosures on 8,796 loans made for a total of seventy-million dollars.

We believe the FHA and GI loan programs have been very successful and have enabled many to become home owners that otherwise would not have been able to obtain the financing. In the latter years the terms on FHA and GI loans have been liberalized; we feel perhaps they are too liberal. Loans have been made for as long as thirty-five years with a small down payment. We have not been enthusiastic about the new liberal terms, and we have tried to hold them down. Competition has made it necessary to take longer terms than we like, and this is perhaps the reason for a larger number of foreclosures.

Neither we nor any investor to whom we have sold mortgages has ever taken a loss, except some expenses in connection with the foreclosure. On FHA mortgages foreclosed, the United States Government gives us United States Bonds for the amount owing on the mortgage. Although the bonds are long term, FHA has surplus reserves, and the bonds we have received have been called and paid. Of the houses acquired by FHA, many have been sold by them.

Early in the year we had a stock split, giving two and one-half shares of $10.00 par value stock for each presently outstanding share having a par value of $25.00. The principal object in making the stock split was to enable us to have a lower value on fractional shares resulting from stock dividends. Furthermore, stockholders seem to like to have more shares even though the value of their total investment remains the same. We now have 150,000 shares outstanding.

We continued our interest in automation and knew the day was approaching when we would have to make a decision. In March the First National Bank of the Black Hills ordered equipment produced by Burroughs, and for this we were happy. It meant we did not have to push automation alone. With two banks in automation, there is the advantage on clearings where we will micro ink the amount of the checks for each other. It will also be easier to encourage customers to use micro ink numbered checks when two banks are in automation.

After their purchase the pressure from the salesmen from IBM, NCR, and Burroughs became intense. We spent many hours listening to their presentations. We also took time to visit several installations of automation in other banks. In July we decided to purchase the newest IBM Series 360 model. We wanted to go first class, and since this was the newest equipment on the market, we considered it best suited for us. We expect to purchase the equipment, which means an expenditure of more than four hundred thousand dollars.

The IBM 360 series is so new that delivery will not be made until late 1965. We therefore decided to lease the IBM 1440 model until the 360 is available. We took everyone by surprise by bringing in the IBM Sorter-Reader in October. We installed it in our bank lobby, where the public could see it work. The checks flying into the pockets created much interest.

The day we decided to purchase the IBM equipment, we called our whole staff together to tell them what our plans were. We wanted them to have first-hand information. I think it is wrong when an officer or employee first hears about something at the bank on the street or reads it in the newspapers. We also told our employees that no one would lose his job because of automation.

Although we expect our staff will be reduced, we know normal resignations during the year will take care of it.

I was in New York attending the American Bankers Association Automation Conference when the following telegram was received at the bank:

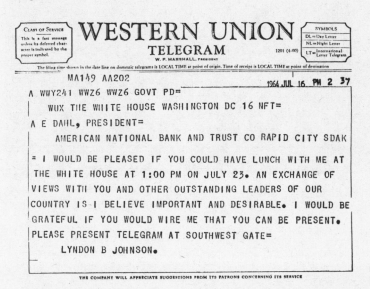

| CLASS OF SERVICE | WESTERN UNION | SYMBOLS |
| This is a fast message unless its deferred character is indicated by the proper symbol. | TELEGRAM | DL=Day Letter NL=Night Letter LT=International Letter Telegram |

The filing time shown in the date line on domestic telegrams is LOCAL TIME at point of origin. Time of receipt is LOCAL TIME at point of destination

MA149 AA202   1964 JUL 16 PM 2 37

A WWY241 WWZ6 WWZ6 GOVT PD=

WUX THE WHITE HOUSE WASHINGTON DC 16 NFT=

A E DAHL, PRESIDENT=

AMERICAN NATIONAL BANK AND TRUST CO RAPID CITY SDAK

= I WOULD BE PLEASED IF YOU COULD HAVE LUNCH WITH ME AT THE WHITE HOUSE AT 1:00 PM ON JULY 23. AN EXCHANGE OF VIEWS WITH YOU AND OTHER OUTSTANDING LEADERS OF OUR COUNTRY IS I BELIEVE IMPORTANT AND DESIRABLE. I WOULD BE GRATEFUL IF YOU WOULD WIRE ME THAT YOU CAN BE PRESENT. PLEASE PRESENT TELEGRAM AT SOUTHWEST GATE=

LYNDON B JOHNSON.

THE COMPANY WILL APPRECIATE SUGGESTIONS FROM ITS PATRONS CONCERNING ITS SERVICE

This was a big surprise and an honor I accepted. There were 214 business people in attendance. Besides the President, ten cabinet officers and four other governmental officials were there. The list included forty-one bankers, but I was the only banker from the Ninth Federal Reserve District. Some of the prominent business men present included Henry Ford II, of Ford Motor Company, Roger M. Blough, from the United States Steel Corporation, and many others. How I came to be invited I do not know.

The President shook hands with his guests as we entered a room on the second floor. We were asked to pick a numbered card out of a box and I drew table four. The table seated ten persons, and the host at our table was Robert Kennedy, the Attorney General. He shook

At The White House

Mount Rushmore Memorial

hands with all seated at the table. He was seated on the other side of the large table from me and did all his visiting with the man sitting next to him, whom I did not know.

The menu, printed on a stiff card with the gold Presidential seal at the top, consisted of: Melon and Prosuitte, Breast of Chicken, Mexican Rice Pilaff, Green Beans Amandine, and Strawberry Bombe Glace. Words like these are not familiar to me, but the food was good.

There was no head table, but the President was sitting at a table in the center of the room. He introduced all his Cabinet Officers and jokingly remarked that this was the first time he had all his Cabinet Officers present for some time.

After the luncheon, we all passed to the other end of the White House. The President stood on the platform waiting for all to be seated. Naturally there was a lot of noise from people visiting, but when the President spoke, I have never before seen a group of people become quiet so suddenly. After a few words of greeting, he introduced successively Mr. Robert S. McNamara, the Secretary of Defense; Mr. Dean Rusk, the Secretary of State; and Adlai Stevenson from the United Nations. Each spoke briefly.

The President then spoke for about a half hour, using some charts to illustrate his points. He talked principally about the prosperity of the country and gains during the time he had been President. He asked if there were any questions. There were three, but none of any importance.

It was now four o'clock and the meeting adjourned. The President quickly went to the door and shook hands with all of us in parting. It was a very interesting experience.

On October 6 my good friend Harry Herbst and I decided to take a vacation trip to Europe. We arrived in London within fifteen hours after departure from

Rapid City. Our next stop was Berlin, and one afternoon we took a taxi for a four-hour tour of East Berlin.
We had no difficulty with our passports entering or returning. It was an interesting experience and we spent
most of our time driving around the city and taking
pictures. The few automobiles and people on the streets
were in great contrast to busy West Berlin. We then
flew to Munich, Milan, Nice, and to Paris, and returned
home from there.

On December 5 the stockholders voted our ninth
stock dividend of $100,000.00 increasing our capital to
$1,600,000.00. The directors transferred a like amount
from undivided profits to surplus fund, resulting in a
surplus fund of equal amount. The number of shares
was increased to 160,000.

The American National Bank and Trust Company
is owned by two hundred six stockholders. The directors
and their families own 106,890 shares, or 66.8 per cent
of the outstanding stock. The employees and the profit
sharing fund own 12,167 shares, or 7.6 per cent of the
stock. The total of both equals 119,057 shares, or 74.4
per cent of the total shares outstanding.

On December 31 we paid our fiftieth cash dividend
to our stockholders. In the early years we paid dividends
on an annual basis, but since 1944 they have been paid
on a semi-annual basis. At first our capital was small
so the dividend was not large. Since it was necessary to
build capital accounts, our dividends have always been
on a conservative basis, with a payout of about one-
fourth of our earnings. The first year was a short year
and no dividend was paid, but every year thereafter we
have paid dividends without interruption, steadily increasing the amount of the dividend without any reduction. Our total dividends paid now amount to $1,262,-
965.00. Here is the record:

Year	Amount	Year	Amount
1935	$ 2,000.00	1950	$ 48,000.00
1936	2,115.00	1951	48,000.00
1937	2,135.00	1952	48,000.00
1938	2,165.00	1953	48,000.00
1939	2,200.00	1954	50,000.00
1940	2,500.00	1955	50,000.00
1941	2,500.00	1956	50,000.00
1942	4,000.00	1957	50,000.00
1943	5,000.00	1958	55,000.00
1944	6,000.00	1959	60,000.00
1945	12,000.00	1960	60,000.00
1946	15,000.00	1961	64,000.00
1947	32,000.00	1962	95,350.00
1948	32,000.00	1963	116,000.00
1949	32,000.00	1964	122,000.00

Total Dividends Paid	$1,117,965.00
Dividends paid by Western National	32,000.00
Dividends paid by R. C. Trust Co.	113,000.00
	$1,262,965.00

As we noted before, the Western National Bank and the Rapid City Trust Company, both affiliate banks, were merged into the American National Bank and Trust Company in 1962. The above figures include the dividends paid by them during their years of operation.

The maximum rate of interest a bank may pay on savings deposits is regulated by the Federal Reserve Board. During the last few years the maximum rate has been successively raised by the board. This year the rate was raised to four and one-half per cent. I think this rate is too high, and so far no bank in Rapid City and this area has raised their rates. Whenever a bank pays a high rate of interest to its depositors, it must offset the increased expense in some way. One method is to raise the rate of interest on loans, but whenever we charge the borrowers an excessive rate, we are not doing our community any good, and we may retard expansion, curtail building, and interfere with progress. Another method is to expand the loan volume, and in so doing lower the quality of the loans in order to obtain the loans. On top of this the bank becomes less liquid, and probably less profitable and less able to take care of losses that may occur in any bank. The salary expense used to be the largest expense in a bank. Today in many banks the interest paid is the largest expense, and to some banks it is becoming burdensome. I still feel that customers are more interested in doing business with a strong, profitable bank than in the amount of interest the bank pays. To be strong, a bank must be profitable so that it has an adequate margin to take care of any losses that may occur, as well as to be able to take proper care of the community it serves.

Competitively over the thirty-one years the American National Bank and Trust Company has done very well. In Rapid City business we are far in the lead. Since all three banks in Rapid City operate branches out of town, the deposits for Rapid City are not published separately. We have other information that proves our dominance in Rapid City business.

For many years we have counted the checks deposited by two utilities and one large department store, dividing them among the three banks. The count of checks from the three firms divided among the banks runs very close. Below is the average percentage of checks drawn on this bank:

	Checks Drawn on American National	Checks Drawn on Other Two Banks
Year 1963	57.9%	42.1%
Year 1964	58.3%	41.7%

Every month we report to the Federal Reserve Bank the total dollar amount of checks charged to our customers' account, and this is called Bank Debits. The report from the Federal Reserve Bank, which is also given in the newspapers, shows the total bank debits for Rapid City, and a comparison with the previous years. It is then a matter of subtraction to arrive at the percentage bank debits handled by this bank. The figures for the past two years are:

Total Bank Debits All Three Banks		
Year 1963	$819,394,000	100%
Year 1964	$767,870,000	100%
Total Bank Debits American National		
Year 1963	$441,466,000	53.9%
Year 1964	$433,565,000	56.5%
Total Bank Debits Other Two Banks		
Year 1963	$377,928,000	46.1%
Year 1964	$334,214,000	43.5%

Bank debits decreased in 1964 over the previous year, but the drop in bank debits at the American National Bank was only 1.8 per cent compared with a drop of 11.5 per cent in the other two banks.

We think it is safe to say that fifty-eight per cent of the people in Rapid City do their business with this bank. The American National is truly "A Bank Built by Customers." Our branch in Sturgis during the year 1964 had 68.42 per cent of the bank debits for Sturgis, and our branch in Hot Springs had 40.10 per cent of the bank debits for Hot Springs, the latter branch being a little more than four years old.

We had another good year, better than we had expected, and I think our progress is best illustrated by the annual report for the year-end presented to the stockholders of the bank, so here it is in full:

AMERICAN NATIONAL BANK AND TRUST COMPANY

Rapid City, South Dakota

January 12, 1965

To the Stockholders:

We are pleased to present our thirty-first annual report. The year has been a good one with net earnings above the previous year.

Gross earnings from all sources amounted to $3,169,024.23. Net income before taxes were $927,689.19, a figure less than last year. Due to lower Federal Income Taxes, and with a larger holding of muncipal bonds, the interest from which is tax exempt, the net earnings after applicable taxes were greater than last year. They amounted to $515,348.03 equal to $3.22 per share, compared with $499,418.93 and $3.12 per share, the previous year.

Profits resulting from bond maturities and sales amounted to $20,603.37. After deducting $5,158.84 taxes, the net profit of $15,444.53 was credited directly to undivided profits.

The transfer to Reserve for Losses account was $100,000.00, the maximum amount allowable under the freeze of the Internal Revenue Department. The total now in this account is $1,022,738.25. The transfer resulted in a tax saving of $50,000.00.

On December 10, 1964 a stock dividend of $100,000.00 was paid increasing the Capital to $1,600,-000.00. This is the ninth stock dividend declared since the bank was organized. Another $100,000.00 was transferred to Surplus Account.

Total capital funds now total $5,069,827.83, as follows: Capital, $1,600,000.00; Surplus $1,600,-000.00; Undivided Profits $765,772.56; Reserve for Losses $1,022,738.25; and Surplus in Building Corporation $81,317.02

Dividends paid in 1964 amounted to $132,000.00. Dividends were increased on December 31st, to an annual rate of ninety cents a share compared to eighty cents previously paid. The dividend payout for 1964 amounted to 24.73%, a conservative amount. The balance was used to build capital accounts. We now have the largest capital funds to deposits in the history of the bank.

The American Building Corporation is wholly owned by the American National Bank and Trust Company. The carrying value of the bank buildings owned are conservatively valued. Where possible the double depreciation is taken, which results in faster writedown of property. It reduces the earnings now but will result in increased earnings in later years. The loan of $280,000.00 is carried by the First National Bank of Minneapolis on an unsecured basis. We can reduce this debt about $50,000.00 a year.

The book value of your stock using the figures for capital, surplus and undivided profits amount to $24.78 per share. The Surplus in the American Building Corporation will add $.51 per share. The reserve for losses amounts to $6.39 per share, for a total book value of $31.68 per share. If taxes are applied to the reserve for losses account it will amount to $3.20 per share, and reduce the book value to $28.48 per share. Since there is more than one way to figure book values, you may take your choice.

The deposits at the year end amount to $54,444,590.32 compared with $51,635,990.31 a year ago. Loans total $28,117,446.63 compared with $28,363,856.16 the previous year.

We have received our automation equipment. Presently we are installing the IBM 1440 series, but this will be replaced by the newest, fastest IBM 360 series which will be available in about a year. The conversion cost will be expensive, and at this time it is hard to tell what effect it will have on the earnings for 1965. Automation will stabilize our costs and should reduce our costs in the future.

In behalf of the Board of Directors, most sincerely,

Chairman of Board   President

COMPARATIVE EARNINGS REPORT

INCOME

	Year 1962	Year 1963	Year 1964
Interest on Loans	$1,517,657.70	$1,939,206.14	$1,972,975.00
Interest on United States Bonds	603,759.84	560,258.36	535,565.11
Interest on Municipal Securities	7,601.91	30,321.93	106,656.44
Interest and Dividends, Other Securities	15,056.66	11,904.62	39,052.13
Activity Charges on Accounts	251,200.53	260,307.66	269,031.93
Mortgage Servicing Fees	158,058.71	153,206.98	141,717.66
Trust and Escrow Fees	51,850.09	49,627.56	52,860.98
Other Income	61,720.70	57,804.91	51,164.98
Total Income	$2,666,906.14	$3,062,638.16	$3,169,024.23

EXPENSES

	Year 1962	Year 1963	Year 1964
Interest Paid	$ 625,635.43	$ 779,200.97	$ 895,865.03
Salaries	571,642.09	648,433.42	702,665.96
Profit Sharing Contribution	58,707.84	64,605.31	71,274.29
Depreciation Equipment	68,410.77	61,064.82	54,973.15
Other Expenses	436,151.64	510,753.61	513,412.70
Total Expenses	1,760,547.77	2,064,058.13	2,238,191.13
Operating Profit	906,358.37	998,580.03	930,833.10
Additions to Income	3,811.08	7,183.32	2,561.15
Less Losses and Other Deductions	9,706.80	13,058.83	5,705.06
Net Income	900,462.65	992,704.52	927,689.19
Less Income Taxes Applicable to Net Earnings	451,395.23	493,285.59	412,341.16
Net Profit After Taxes	449,067.42	499,418.93	515,348.03
Operating Earnings Per Share	2.80	3.12	3.22

RECONCILEMENT OF CAPITAL FUNDS

	1962	1963	1964
Capital Funds, Beginning of Year	$2,540,025.30	$3,317,905.85	$3.616,980.00
Additions:			
Net Profit from Above	449,067.42	499,418.93	515,348.03
Tax Credit Transfer Res. for Losses	100,321.24	127,131.80	50,000.00
Bond Profit less applicable taxes		38,523.42	15,444.53
Merger Credit Sturgis	531,841.89		
Deductions:			
Transfer to Reserve for Losses	200,000.00	250,000.00	100,000.00
Dividends Paid	103,350.00	116,000.00	132,000.00
Capital Funds, End of Year	$3,317,905.85	$3,616,980.00	$3,965,772.56

COMPARATIVE STATEMENTS

AMERICAN BUILDING CORPORATION
Rapid City, South Dakota

ASSETS

	Dec. 31, 1962	Dec. 31, 1963	Dec. 31, 1964
Cash on Hand	$ 2,056.91	$ 1,620.19	$ 3,918.27
Prepaid Insurance	1,681.75	1,777.92	1,777.76
American National Bank Building, less depreciation	633,964.81	608,826.21	595,289.68
Auto Bank, Parking Lot, less depreciation	145,557.08	139,275.93	133,971.30
Northeast Branch Building, less depreciation	83,552.62	79,828.04	78,321.69
Hot Springs Branch Building, less depreciation	44,458.39	41,541.41	38,624.43
Sturgis Branch Building less depreciation	58,549.17	231,968.48	225,313.16
Equipment Owned, less depreciation	280.20	530.18	112.00
	$ 970,100.93	$1,105,368.36	$1,077,328.29

LIABILITIES AND CAPITAL

	Dec. 31, 1962	Dec. 31, 1963	Dec. 31, 1964
Unsecured Notes	$ 310,000.00	$ 330,000.00	$ 280,000.00
Accounts Payable		7,521.00	
Contract Payable on Northeast Branch	78,200.73	75,512.11	72,657.67
Reserve for Accrued Real Estate Taxes	24,795.25	25,472.82	29,261.52
Reserve for Interest Accrued Payable	197.41	290.00	6,811.88
Reserve for Income Taxes Payable	2,180.23	3,535.62	7,280.20
Capital Stock Owned by American National Bank	500,000.00	600,000.00	600,000.00
Earned Surplus	54,727.31	63,036.81	81,317.02
	$ 970,100.93	$1,105,368.36	$1,077,328.29

COMPARATIVE EARNINGS STATEMENT

	Year 1962	Year 1963	Year 1964
Rental Income	$ 118,527.99	$ 128,508.46	$ 147,858.56
Less Expenditure of			
Utilities	7,264.05	6,412.10	4,733.72
Insurance	2,110.69	2,245.64	2,341.18
Repairs & Maintenance	9,097.90	9,347.11	8,415.36
Property Taxes	24,455.49	25,531.14	29,261.52
Interest Paid	17,592.55	18,925.67	18,567.32
Depreciation	49,446.49	52,490.00	57,104.12
Miscellaneous Expense	1,152.36	1,686.17	1,874.93
Total Expense	$ 111,119.53	$ 116,637.83	$ 122,298.15
Net Profit	7,408.46	11,870.63	25,560.41
Less Income Taxes	2,180.23	3,561.13	7,280.20
Net Addition to Surplus	5,228.23	8,309.50	18,280.21
Earnings per share of American National Bank	.03	.05	.11

BOARD OF DIRECTORS

Standing: *Fred Barth, Ivan Landstrom, C. G. Skartvedt,*
Clark Carnaby, B. J. Roskos, Russell Halvorson.
Seated: *W. E. Shoberg, A. E. Dahl, Walter Pailing, H. J.*
Devereaux, Earl Keller.

Our Official Staff

42

Nineteen Sixty Five

On January 4 we received all our automation equipment from IBM. A few days later we commenced posting our checking accounts on automation, one book at a time. We have ten books covering about 15,000 accounts in our main office. We run parallel for a few days on the first book only. It worked so nicely we discontinued the parallel runs. We added a book every three days to correspond with the cycling of our monthly statements, and by February 15 all our books were on automation. The equipment has worked very well.

We had not planned to be first with automation in Rapid City since our competition had ordered their equipment four months before we did. The reason we were first to receive and process our demand deposit accounts on automation was that our people were ready, and the equipment was available. At the time we placed our order with IBM we made a condition that it was subject to finding us a very experienced man to operate the equipment. They put us in touch with a former South

Dakotan, who was with a large data center in Milwaukee. He has had ten years of experience with automation, and to him it was a simple matter to program and place the equipment in operation. We also sent three of our own employees to IBM school at Minneapolis to assist him. In November, after he returned from Minneapolis to try out his programs at the IBM center, he came to me and said he was ready. It was then a matter of waiting for the equipment, which arrived in January. We expect to have our installment loans on automation soon and we now have the program ready. It makes no difference how much a bank spends on automation or other equipment, we still have to have people with more brains than the computer to operate it. In this respect, our planning was good and it has paid us well to obtain an experienced man to head this department.

The trust department of our bank is now more than ten years old. The growth of this department has not been spectacular but it has been steady. Unlike many other communities where trust departments have been established for many years, people of this community were not familiar with the many services a trust department can perform for them. Nevertheless this department has grown to where we now administer assets valued near ten million dollars.

With full appreciation of the great responsibility placed on the bank in properly administering trusts, we employed two very experienced men to manage this department and they have done a very commendable job. Two years ago this department set up two common trust funds. Fund A is a growth fund with investments in nationally known common stocks. Fund B is an income fund with investments in bonds and preferred stocks. The common trust fund enables the small trust to enjoy the diversification and income possibilities that large trusts have. The total assets in the common trust funds are approaching two million dollars, which we understand is the largest of such funds in South Dakota.

We have probated several estates. We have many guardianships, trusts, including profit-sharing trusts. This department also handles our escrows. We look forward to the day when the trust assets will equal the assets of the bank.

Before I close this book I am going to say something about group and branch banking. This is a hot subject in many states, so perhaps some observations on this subject may be of interest. South Dakota has both group banking and branch banking in a greater measure than most states. I feel that the people of this state are satisfied with the services rendered by the banks of South Dakota, whether they are group, branch, or independent banks. We have a very large number of independent banks of all sizes operating side by side with the group banks and banks with branches that are excellent banks doing an excellent job in banking, and I believe none has been hurt by either group banking or branch banking.

South Dakota has 33 national banks operating 35 branches, and 140 state banks operating 36 branches and offices, for a total of 173 banks and 71 branches. This makes 244 banking offices in the state.

Total deposits in South Dakota banks on Dec. 31, 1964 amounted to $986,639,563.00. Five banks, all operating branches, have deposits of more than fifty million dollars. Four of the banks are group banks, and the American National Bank is the only bank outside the group banks with more than fifty million dollars in deposits. The largest bank in South Dakota has eighty-four million in deposits.

The next largest bank, after the five mentioned above, an independent bank, had deposits of forty million dollars deposits. Twelve have deposits of ten to twenty-five million dollars in deposits. Twenty-one banks have deposits of five to ten million. One hundred and twenty-one banks have deposits of one to five million dollars. We have thirteen banks with less than one million deposits. South Dakota has a great many independent banks. They have all prospered and served their communities well.

The largest amount of deposits is held by the Northwest Bancorporation group, operating four banks with twenty-three branches, with deposits totaling $231,521,-463.00 or 23.5 per cent of the state's deposits. The First Bank Stock Corporation group, consisting of seven banks with eight branches, have deposits of $101,637,869.00 equal to 10.3 per cent of the deposits in the state. Third is the American National Bank and Trust Company with four branches and $54,444,590.00 or 5.5 per cent of the deposits in the state.

South Dakota has had state-wide branch banking for more than thirty years. The first law permitting branches was enacted at a special session of the legislature in 1933. This law provided that only banks with more than $100,00.00 capital could have branches. This was a shotgun law quickly passed without hearings or opposition to help solve the problems of certain national banks in the state.

This law was of little value to the many small state banks in the state that did not have the capital requirements. So, at the next regular session of the legislature in January, 1935, an additional law was enacted relating to the establishment of offices, limiting the office to accepting deposits, issuing drafts, making change, and paying checks. This enabled many smaller banks to open offices in bankless towns and was of great benefit to the banks and bankless communities.

We have a good branch bank law in South Dakota for the protection of the smaller banks. No branch may be established in any town or city of less than 3,000 population if the community has one bank or established

Around The World

Our New Home 1965

branch. No branch can be established in a city with a population between 3,000 and 15,000 people if the city now is served by two banks or branches. The only way a branch may be established in these cities is by the purchase or merger of an existing bank in the ctiy. In cities with a population over 15,000 there is no limitation or restrictions.

Branch banking has been successful in South Dakota. There is no enmity between banks, whether they be group, branch or independent banks. I have never heard any criticism from the public about either group or branch banking, and there has never been any demand for the repeal of the law. I know from my own experience that if another bank can serve our customers better, they give no concern as to who owns the bank, whether it is a group bank, a branch or main office, or if it is an independent bank.

I have lived in many homes during my lifetime. For the past eighteen years we have enjoyed living in our home on West Boulevard. As a person grows older he loses his interest in taking care of the lawn and doing chores around a home, and the wife should not be burdened with the care of a large home. I have, for the past few years, had some enthusiasm for a nice apartment, but I could not interest anyone in building one. So this year, in partnership with some friends of ours, we decided to build a twenty-four unit deluxe seven-story apartment house near downtown. My wife and I are looking forward to moving into the apartment on the top floor by this fall.

My greatest pleasure over the years has been traveling. When we lived in Toronto, Castlewood, and during the first years in Rapid City, the three of us, Verley, her mother and I, managed to take the car and make some trips together. I remember spending vacations in New York, Los Angeles, Seattle, New Orleans, and traveling shorter distances to other cities. We used to stay at tourist homes for $2.00 a night and we ate at the Woolworth counter to save money. We covered many miles with little expense.

I have been interested in photography. Years ago I took pictures, developed them, and often made enlargements. I have always taken colored pictures, and in later years that has been the extent of my interest in photography. I have owned many cameras. I have thousands of colored slides and a photographic history of our families. On our trips to Europe and around the world I took hundreds of pictures in color.

In recent years travel has again been our chief interest. Some trips have been for business and others for pleasure. In the last five years I have flown about 180,000 miles, and on many occasions my wife has accompanied me.

Movies, radio and TV interest me very little today, and unless there is a news program or sports, particularly baseball, I do not turn on the radio or watch TV. I like to read, but my eyes are not strong, so I confine my reading mostly to newspapers, trade magazines and weekly news magazines.

At the time I married I had no interest in cards. My wife taught me to play bridge, and we especially enjoy duplicate bridge. It has given us something to do, and it is something in which we have a mutual interest. Since my eyes will not permit extensive reading and I do not care to watch TV, duplicate bridge has been an outlet that helped us to spend many pleasant evenings. We do not let bridge interfere with social activities. If some friends are kind enough to invite us to spend an evening with them, we always pass up bridge.

Usually an evening at duplicate bridge lasts about four hours, after which we have coffee and refreshments. No one plays for money, but every duplicate player plays to earn points. When a player earns 300 points, 250 of which may be won in local duplicate sessions and

50 points in tournament play, he receives a gold card with the title of Life Master. Most people never achieve this goal because they do not have the opportunity to attend tournaments. In the United States a little more than 5,000 Life Master Cards have been issued over the past thirty years. How many are living, I do not know, but perhaps a good guess would be about 3,500. I am proud that my wife has the necessary points and is now a Life Master.

The success I may have had has been due to many things — my parents, my family, my associates in the bank — but there are four men to whom I owe much, who gave me the opportunities that came my way.

First was Lyman Fries, cashier of the First National Bank of Toronto, South Dakota, who offered me my first job in a bank and gave me the opportunity to become a banker. He let me take responsibility and do many things around a small bank that gave me the fundamentals of banking. He is now deceased.

Second was Carl N. Halvorson, cashier of the Citizens State Bank of Castlewood, South Dakota, who gave me my second job in a bank. He was a perfectionist and everything had to be done right, which was good training for me. He too is deceased.

Third is E. A. Ruden, former Superintendent of Banks for South Dakota, who gave me the position of bank examiner. This was most valuable experience. Later he offered me the position of receiver of the Pennington County Bank, which brought me to Rapid City. This position gave me valuable experience and enabled me to become acquainted with the men that led to the organization of this bank. He now lives in Brookings, South Dakota.

Finally I want to mention Roy Dean. He was the man who led the fight for local liquidation and brought me back to Rapid City after I was fired by the banking department. He was also the father of the idea of organizing the Rapid City National Bank, and had an important part in opening the bank, which gave me the position of managing officer of this bank. Roy has since passed away.

So as we pass through this life it is important — perhaps sometimes it seems just lucky — to be at the right place at the right time, and to have the opportunity to succeed. The men I have mentioned had much to do with shaping my life, and to them I am very grateful.

To my associates I owe much. I have been fortunate in having the finest and most capable group of officers and staff in the banking business in this bank. Today they manage the bank. They work as a team and they make decisions, large and small. Whenever I am away from the bank, which has been more frequent in the later years, I do not have any worry. I know they are capable of doing a good job at all times.

Training men and women to take responsibility is important. I like to give officers much authority, and then it is up to them to sink or swim. I do not want to be bothered with details. I do not want to look over their shoulders and watch everything they do. If they make a mistake I do not criticize them. They perhaps feel worse than I do, and they learn from the mistakes they make. If they need help I am always glad to give it. My office door is always open and they can feel free to come in and discuss their problems.

It has been a pleasure to me to see the men and women in this bank grow in stature and become capable bankers. I like to see the people on our staff assume responsibility and take initiative. They will not always be right, but if they know the fundamentals, they will be right most of the time. Avoiding tough problems will not get a man anywhere. The development of instinctive ability to make quick and accurate decisions is important. I have always made quick decisions, pos-

265

Agnes and I Boarding Airplane

TORGERSONS
Richard   Verley   Harris   Dianne

BINDERS
Ray   Sandra   Terry   James

sibly sometimes too quick, but over the years I have found that usually my first decision is as good as the one I have mulled over for a week. Customers, too, like quick, decisive actions. I think the borrower would rather have a quick answer, even if it is "no," than to wait a week to have a "yes" answer from his banker. The more knowledgeable a person is the better his decisions. Many of our officers and staff have been with this bank so many years that they find it easy to make decisions. I have great faith in the young men and women on their way up. They have a keener and sharper mind than I have today.

No bank officers have worked harder than our officers. They have worked together as one happy official family. We have never had any problem of office politics. There has been no backbiting or undermining of one another on the part of the officers and staff. They have always shown great respect for one another.

My office is located in the front part of the building between the two entrances, with windows facing the street. It is a large, comfortable office. Between my office and the bank lobby are large glass panels from the floor to the ceiling, enabling me to sit at my desk and see the people in the lobby and in most of the officers' section.

One of my pleasures now is having people drop into my office for a visit. Often some old timers, whom I have not seen for some time, will stop by to say hello and reminisce about the past. I often greet people passing by my office by waving to them.

Just outside the door on the glass I have my name and title, and underneath the words "Come in." I never close the door unless I have a conference, but I have a pushbutton on my desk that will electrically draw the drapes shut for complete privacy if the customer likes.

One day a man standing out in the lobby a little way from my office came up and looked at the words "Come in." He remarked that was "kind of cute," and asked me who Mr. Dahl was. I told him it was me. After a brief conversation he left.

So, as I sit at my desk in my office and pound out the last paragraph of this autobiography of a banker, I will repeat the first line in the book. "I have had a full, interesting and rewarding life." I am very fortunate, for although I am now sixty-eight years old, I am still in good health. I enjoy my family and friends. I have an interest in the happenings of the day. I enjoy coming to the bank in the morning and look forward to an interesting day. So I do not plan to retire.

Appendix

GROWTH IN ASSETS

(in thousands)

Year	Cash	U.S. Bds	Mun. Bds.	Loans	Bk & Fix	Other	Total
1934	$ 437	$ 90	$ 131	$ 166	$ 31	$ 10	$ 865
1935	515	267	151	395	30	12	1,370
1936	752	293	272	631	30	16	1,994
1937	768	251	270	770	32	13	2,104
1938	863	240	270	1,005	32	16	2,428
1939	1,065	106	352	1,244	31	21	2,819
1940	1,365	118	322	1,380	30	25	3,240
1941	1,137	186	325	1,776	72	26	3,522
1942	2,277	2,062	431	1,503	168	28	6,469
1943	1,911	3,350	623	1,594	164	38	7,680
1944	3,014	3,270	574	1,495	165	39	8,557
1945	3,951	4,644	507	1,917	159	41	11,219
1946	3,260	4,923	450	3,125	159	48	11,965
1947	3,140	5,449	499	4,094	155	44	13,661
1948	4,129	4,717	510	4,795	170	53	14,374
1949	3,951	5,632	457	5,038	167	71	15,317
1950	3,993	5,768	390	5,866	172	71	16,260
1951	4,809	7,439	297	5,427	168	87	18,227
1952	4,768	8,317	224	6,038	170	113	19,630
1953	5,188	7,358	217	7,174	287	115	20,339
1954	4,473	8,361	49	8,684	311	124	22,002
1955	5,068	8,892	87	9,117	306	137	23,616
1956	5,135	8,320	133	11,314	303	174	25,379
1957	5,624	10,571	92	11,671	353	247	28,558
1958	5,730	12,266	73	14,026	345	264	32,704
1959	6,043	10,132	92	16,875	540	410	34,092
1760	5,903	12,005	63	16,444	739	381	35,535
1961	7,416	14,650	79	19,546	704	445	42,840
1962	8,990	16,148	433	27,016	771	549	53,907
1963	7,185	17,259	2,334	29,334	866	624	57,602
1964	10,259	15,710	4,185	29,140	841	523	60,658

GROWTH IN DEPOSITS AND CAPITAL
(in thousands)

	Deposits	Prf. Cap.	Com. Cap.	Surplus	Und. Prfs.	Res. Loss	Reserve
1934	$ 741	$ 50	$ 50	$ 20	$ 1	$	$ 3
1935	1,229	50	50	21	8		12
1936	1,837	47	53	25	11		16
1937	1,925	46	54	40	18		21
1938	2,221	46	54	60	22		25
1939	2,573	45	55	75	47		24
1940	2,893	100	100	78	35		34
1941	3,194	50	100	125	20		33
1942	6,126	50	100	150	20		23
1943	7,299	50	100	150	51		30
1944	8,138		150	200	33		36
1945	10,757		150	200	63		49
1946	11,419		200	200	74		72
1947	12,982		200	300	40	27	112
1948	13,580		200	300	103	36	155
1949	14,363		200	400	101	48	206
1950	15,147		200	400	184	67	260
1951	17,004		200	500	163	82	278
1952	18,124		500	420	160	83	343
1953	18,718		500	420	244	78	379
1954	20,275		600	525	129	116	357
1955	21,722		600	525	241	154	374
1956	22,981		700	600	413	193	492
1957	25,913		700	700	459	242	544
1958	29,745		800	800	421	312	626
1959	30,666		1,000	1,000	204	454	768
1960	32,073		1,000	1,000	334	516	612
1961	38,868		1,000	1,000	515	623	834
1962	48,522		1,400	1,400	518	792	1,275
1963	51,636		1,500	1,500	617	970	1,379
1964	54,444		1,600	1,600	766	1,023	1,225

ONE STOCKHOLDER'S INVESTMENT

The stockholders of the American National Bank and Trust Company have profited handsomely on their investments. One of our stockholders died recently and his stock was sold by the executor of his will on bids. Here is a record of his purchases, stock dividends, stock splits, and dividends received:

Year		Cost	Stock Div.	Total Shares	Cash Div.
1934	Purchased 5 shares @ $35.00	$175.00		5	$ 5.00
1935				5	5.00
1936				5	5.00
1937				5	5.00
1938				5	5.00
1939				5	5.00
1940			5	10	12.50
1941				10	12.50
1942				10	20.00
1943				10	20.00
1944	Purchased 5 shares @ $25.00	125.00		15	30.00
1945				15	30.00
1946			5	20	40.00
1847				20	80.00
1948				20	80.00
1949				20	80.00
1950				20	120.00
1951				20	120.00
1952	Bought 14 sh. Rapid City Tr. Co.	420.00	20	40	120.00
1953				40	120.00
1954			10	50	125.00
1955				50	125.00
1956	Bought 10 sh. Western Nat'l for	500.00		50	125.00
1957				50	125.00
1958			10	60	150.00
1959			20	80	150.00
1960				80	150.00
1961				80	150.00
1962	Merg. RCT & WNB rec. 23 sh.			103	206.00
1963			18	131	234.00
1964	Stock split 2½ sh. for 1 share			327	234.00

Total Cash dividends received	$ 2,694.00
Total Dividends paid by Rapid City Trust Company	381.50
Total Dividends paid by Western National Bank	85.00
327 shares sold in 1964 at $41.10	13,439.70
Total received from sale, plus dividends	$16,600.20
Less Cost of shares from above	1,220.00
NET GAIN ON INVESTMENT	**$15,380.20**

OFFICIAL STAFF

	Years With American	Total Years in Banking
A. E. Dahl, Chairman of Board	31	48
Walter Pailing, President	31	31
COMMERCIAL LOAN DEPARTMENT		
W. E. Shoberg, Senior Vice President	31	44
Russell Halvorson, Vice President	16	16
Carl Bangert, Vice President and Cashier	14	16
MORTGAGE LOAN DEPARTMENT		
Earl L. Keller, Senior Vice President	31	39
Lucille Crow, Assistant Vice President	25	25
Walter Linderman, Assistant Vice President	7	7
INSTALLMENT LOAN DEPARTMENT		
Lyle Welsh, Vice President	10	10
Robert Bock, Assistant Cashier	5	5
Frank McCormick, Assistant Cashier	2	2
TRUST DEPARTMENT		
Clark Carnaby, Vice President	4	11
William Kilroy, Vice President	8	15
PUBLIC RELATIONS DEPARTMENT		
Ronald J. Campbell, Vice President	5	25
Frances Vincent, Vice President	31	31
AUDITING AND AUTOMATION		
Lewis Rohrer, Assistant Vice President	5	8
James Bertelsen, Assistant Vice President	1	1
Ted Mrnak, Assistant Cashier	3	9
TRAVEL DEPARTMENT		
Al McDonald, Manager	4	4
NORTHEAST OFFICE		
Lloyd Klaudt, Assistant Vice President	7	12
Gideon Stroh, Assistant Cashier	8	8
WESTERN OFFICE		
Jerry Harder, Assistant Vice President	9	13
Don Lorenzen, Assistant Cashier	3	8
BEAR BUTTE VALLEY OFFICE, STURGIS		
Fred Barth, Vice President	30	35
Bruce Walker, Vice President	3	14
Dan Mayer, Assistant Cashier	6	6
Harold J. Walker, Advisory Director	3	50
HOT SPRINGS OFFICE		
LeRoy Hofer, Assistant Vice President	6	7
Allan Hill, Assistant Cashier	1	1

BANKING IN WESTERN SOUTH DAKOTA

It may be of some historical interest to go back nearly fifty years to review the banking facilities in western South Dakota as it existed at that time. Then there were forty-eight banks in six counties comprising the Black Hills. It was an overbanked situation, with many banks in small towns that could not support a bank. Today there are nine banks with eighteen branches, a total of twenty-seven banking offices. I am indebted to B. W. Keating, retired banker, for the list of banks and their deposits as of the year 1918, the year he started in the banking business.

Pennington County Bank, Rapid City (1)	$1,214,652.00
Security Savings Bank, Rapid City (1)	398,942.00
First National Bank of Rapid City (2)	1,167,556.00
Merchants Loan and Trust Company (1)	220,201.00
Owanka State Bank, Owanka (1)	132,672.00
First State Bank, Quinn (1)	88,506.00
State Bank of Scenic (1)	51,025.00
Underwood State Bank, New Underwood (3)	167,592.00
First State Bank, Wall (4)	94,476.00
Bank of Wasta (1)	226,972.00
First State Bank, Farmingdale (1)	63,235.00
Hill City Bank (1)	95,078.00
Keystone Bank, Keystone (1)	28,597.00
Custer County Bank, Custer (5)	185,817.00
Buffalo Gap State Bank (6)	117,715.00
First National Bank, Custer (1)	185,716.00
Ranchmans State Bank, Fairburn (1)	66,053.00
Hermosa State Bank (7)	121,067.00
Ardmore State Bank (1)	66,215.00
Bank of Edgemont (1)	329,546.00
Fall River County Bank, Edgemont (1)	116,674.00
Bank of Hot Springs (1)	251,654.00
Stockmans Bank, Hot Springs (1)	329,641.00
People National Bank, Hot Springs (1)	192,618.00
State Bank of Oelrichs (1)	108,925.00
Bear Butte Valley Bank, Sturgis (7)	249,032.00
Commercial National Bank, Sturgis (2)	433,257.00
Farmers State Bank, Faith (5)	271,345.00
Stockmans State Bank, Faith (1)	116,442.00
First State Bank, Piedmont (1)	32,714.00
First State Bank, White Owl (1)	132,672.00
Bank of Spearfish (2)	238,681.00
American National Bank, Spearfish (1)	520,119.00
St. Onge State Bank (1)	85,827.00

Whitewood Banking Company (1)   237,689.00
Black Hills Trust & Savings Bank, Deadwood (1)   455,264.00
First National Bank of Deadwood (2)   1,024,021.00
First National Bank of Lead (8)   1,974,930.00
Miners and Merchants Savings Bank, Lead (5)   292,925.00
Fruitdale State Bank (1)   79,808.00
Irrigators State Bank, Nisland (1)   131,940.00
Reclamation State Bank, Newell (2)   131,169.00
First State Bank, Newell (1)   157,263.00
Livestock Exchange Bank, Newell (1)   68,469.00
Farmers State Bank, Nisland (1)   50,535.00
Butte County Bank, Belle Fourche (2)   748,666.00
First National Bank, Belle Fourche (1)   574,247.00
Belle Fourche State Bank (1)   238,931.00

(1) Liquidated
(2) Merged with First National Bank of the Black Hills
(3) Name changed to First Western Bank and head office moved to Wall
(4) Merged into First Western Bank of Wall
(5) Same bank, same place
(6) Name changed to Southern Hills Bank, and head office moved to Edgemont, with branch at Buffalo Gap
(7) Merged with American National Bank & Trust Company
(8) Name changed to First National Bank of the Black Hills and head office moved to Rapid City

Today western South Dakota is served by a group of strong banks and their branches as follows:

American National Bank & Trust Company, Rapid City with four branches at Hot Springs, Sturgis and two in Rapid City. $54,444,590.32

First National Bank of the Black Hills with nine branches at Lead, Deadwood, Spearfish, Newell, Belle Fourche, Sturgis, Hot Springs, Villa Ranchaero and one in Rapid City.   76,462,139.68

Rushmore State Bank, Rapid City with two branches at Hill City and one in Rapid City.   6,644,395.32

First Western Bank, Wall, with one branch at New Underwood.   4,176.166.00

Custer County Bank, Custer.   3,251,222.00

Southern Hills Bank, Edgemont, with one branch at Buffalo Gap.   2,679,772.00

Farmers State Bank, Faith.   2,475,400.00

Miners & Merchants Bank, Lead   2,455,105.00

Bank of Belle Fourche with one branch at Spearfish   9,250,979.00

Around the World

with Art Dahl

Beirut, Lebanon
Oct. 13, 1963

We had breakfast this Sunday morning at seven o'clock. It was still Saturday at 10 p.m. in Rapid City so we are moving further from home.

We left on a tour to Baalbek, one of Lebanon's touristic highlights. At one time it was a very large city, but today it has a population of 9,000 people. Here the Romans built the largest temple ever built, building over three hundred years with 100,000 slave laborers, and yet never finished it. Today it stands in ruins. The columns, some standing today are the tallest ever erected, the stones the largest ever used, and the form of architecture the most massive ever conceived. They must have had some brilliant architects, engineers, artists and sculptors in the days more than 2000 years ago.

We passed thru the fertile valley of the Promised Land, on to Damascus, the capital of Syria. Syria is a large country but mostly desert. Damascus has a population of 600,000 people. Syria has had fourteen changes of government in three years and our guide says he has been caught with a group of tourists in a revolution five times. Then the first thing they do is to close the border and there is a delay to get out. We all had our visas, and we had to account for the money we took in and out. Nobody trusts anybody and we were checked about three times each way, the last man entering our bus and comparing the photos on the passports with our faces.

We took the city tour of Damascus, and here the old and new world mixes together. Most interesting to me was the old long street, narrow, with shops on both sides, and in the center of the street. Here was merchandise of all kinds. Cuts of meat hanging over the counter, pastries on tables in the street, and all kinds of clothing and novelties. Many people are in western dress but here you see many in Arab or Turkish clothing, men in their headdresses of all kinds, with those bloomer pants where the seat drops down below the knees, the kind you do not see in America. The women with black veils, some in colorful long dresses. Some do not wear shoes, others with flat sandals, high heels and others with old worn out shoes. Children everywhere, friendly and calling "Hello" to you.

We were guided into their church and we were handed the dirtiest worn out sandal coverings to put over our shoes, and I had my trouble to keep them on. The ladies were given black capes.

We covered nearly two hundred miles and returned to the hotel about 10 o'clock, tired and worn out.

Oct. 14, 1963

Today the group left to see the cedars of Lebanon and another long drive. Agnes and I decided we did not want to see all the world on this trip and did not go. We got up late, had a nice breakfast, and walked into the shopping district nearby. No stop lights here and we did our best avoiding the cars. There is a continuous honking of horns, and I am sure the horns wear out before the tires. Our driver yesterday used his horn honking at other cars and pedestrians. He had several kinds of honks and tunes, depending on whether he was passing a car or pretty girl. Here again you can buy anything. Agnes bought a few yards of beautiful gold brocade for a dress. So when you see her in a gold dress, you will know it is Lebanese.

This is the most beautiful hotel I have seen anywhere—the Phoenicia. It is new. We have a large twin bedded room, with nice bath room, with an extra plumbing fixture you do not see in the U.S. There is a swimming pool, coffee shop and newstand which you do not usually see in European hotels.

Yesterday we passed the Arab refugee camp with about a million refugees from Israel. They live in tents and shacks and refuse to work. They think they will return to Israel when the Jews are driven into the ocean. They have waited for 15 years, and will probably wait the rest of their lives. They are supported by a division of the U.N.

Agnes just returned from the hair dresser, wow! Hair puffed up to twice in size. I guess Agnes could not understand Lebanese, and the hair dresser could not understand her. The only thing they both understood was that it cost including tip 15 pounds — about $5.00. It will probably shrink to normal when we get back to Rapid City.

A. E. Dahl, Chairman
AMERICAN NATIONAL BANK
And Trust Company

Around the World

with Art Dahl

Agra, India
Oct. 17, 1963

This morning we drove from New Delhi to Agra by automobile, a distance of 130 miles. Our driver had a 1961 Plymouth. The country was flat. The road was poor by our standards. The driver wore a turban with long hair and beard. He explained he belonged to a religious sect and believed in one God. Our guide was a Hindu. Both spoke good English.

This was an interesting drive. The road was crowded with people, bicycles, carts and trucks. Saw some sugar cane and corn, but no grain. The soil was yellow and dusty, with trees here and there. Lots of cattle in fields, on the streets and along the road. They were black or white, but no Herefords. Also saw goats, water buffaloes. Buildings were poor, and lots of straw huts. An old man had a dancing bear. A few camels and also camel carts. The people were dressed in light clothes in all shapes. Most were barefoot or had sandals. Some of the women had colorful dresses. I believe India has a population of about five hundred million people, and I must have seen a million by this time.

The drive took about four hours, so you see we did not travel very fast due to the large number of people on the road. Parts of the road were being repaired by hand labor and men would carry dirt and rocks in baskets on their heads. India has made progress in education, yet only about 30 per cent have any kind of education.

At Agra we are tonight at Clark's Hotel which is quite new and modern. We have a nice twin bedded room with bath. Four snake charmers entertained outside of the hotel; also a man with three trained birds.

This afternoon we visited the Taj Mahal, a mausoleum in white marble built in 1731 by the ruler Shah Jehan to contain the body of his wife. When he died he was also buried in the mausoleum. It is the outstanding attraction in India and one of the seven wonders of the world. We enjoyed this opportunity to see the Taj Mahal. It is truly beautiful. Our guide told us that it took twenty thousand men 21 years to build it. Again I am amazed at the architects, engineers and organizers that had in old days without the equipment and tools available today. Inside there were beautiful marble screens and decorations, with as many as sixty pieces of marble in a single flower.

In Europe and also here in Agra they have some big slugs of iron attached to your room key, so you will not carry it around. In this hotel it is shaped like the dome of Taj Mahal, and about three inches high and two inches in diameter. It stands nicely on the table with the key dangling on top.

Jaipur, India
Oct. 18, 1963

Today we drove 160 miles from Agra to Jaipur. The hard road was only eight to ten feet wide, enough for one car. Luckily there were few cars on the road, but when we met one, each driver kept the road until about half block away, and then each turned left on the shoulder to pass. It was flat country much like yesterday with many people on the road, and lots of cattle. The guide told us that less than two per cent of the people in India will eat beef. The only salvage when a cow dies is the hide, and the vultures will do the rest.

Here at Jaipur we are at the Rambagh Palace Hotel. At one time it was used as a palace, and since converted into a hotel. We have a room thirty by twenty feet with bath also very large. The food is good but not as fine as in Lebanon and Greece. Ivan and I would like to have a nice thick steak now, but not here.

A group of children posed for a picture and I had about four coins to give them. The children seem to be well behaved and seldom beg, but when they found that I gave some money, they nearly mobbed me. I guess it was not a good idea.

We are tired tonight so this is all today.

A. E. Dahl, Chairman
AMERICAN NATIONAL BANK
And Trust Company

Best In Banking—
At American National

There is no question about it. The American National Bank provides the best checking service in Rapid City. Customers banking here may deposit at any of our four locations in Rapid City at any time. They may choose the Main Office, the Northeast Office, the Western Office or the Auto Bank. An American National check can be used for any office, avoiding all confusion trying to keep each office separate.

The American National also provides seven Drive-in Windows, at three locations, and again our customers have a choice of using the location most convenient. Handy hours too, from eight in the morning to five-thirty in the evening, with two extra hours on Friday.

This bank also provides four After-Hour Depositories at four locations, complete with letter drops everyone may use. Mighty convenient, too.

Customers at the American National Bank have more than 16,000 checking accounts at this bank. In fact, most people in Rapid City bank at the American.

You, too, have a most cordial invitation to join your neighbors and friends who bank at the American National.

Ame
NATIO
and

MAIN OFFICE   WESTERI
701 St. Joe   Baken Park S

STURGIS OFFICE

Member Federal Deposit Insurance Corp

Bank Where Your—
Friends and Neighbors Bank

If you live in Rapid City you will most likely find that most of your friends and neighbors bank at the American National. This is so because most people in Rapid City bank at this bank.

You may ask why so many bank here. Perhaps one of the reasons is that the American National is a bank for everybody. It makes no difference as to the size of your account — you may bank here with the good feeling that your account is appreciated.

Perhaps, too, because we were the first to recognize the need of the individual in introducing new services. For instance, we were the first to provide personal loans and consumer financing. The first to open a mortgage department providing millions for home owners. The first to provide low cost Special Checking Accounts for everybody.

Also important is that the American National is a strong bank thoughtfully managed for you. The American National is owned by home folks, and the officers are the most experienced bankers in town.

It is convenient, too. The American National is located right downtown in the heart of Rapid City. Our Auto Bank and Parking Lot are across the street. Our Northeast office and our Western office are convenient for many.

You, too, have a cordial invitation to bank at the American National Bank.

Mardi Gras tickets available at the Main Office

American
NATIONAL BANK
and Trust Company

MAIN OFFICE   WESTERN OFFICE   NORTHEAST OFFICE
701 St. Joe   Baken Park Shopping Center   301 East North Street

STURGIS OFFICE   HOT SPRINGS OFFICE

Member Federal Deposit Insurance Corporation